PLAN
TO WIN

PLAN TO WIN

Leader's Guide to Creating Breakthrough Business Strategy

Peter von Braun

Order this book online at www.trafford.com
or email orders@trafford.com

Most Trafford titles are also available at major online book retailers.

Printed in the United States of America.

ISBN: 978-1-4907-3996-0 (sc)
ISBN: 978-1-4907-3997-7 (e)

Trafford rev. 06/27/2014

www.trafford.com

North America & international
toll-free: 1 888 232 4444 (USA & Canada)
fax: 812 355 4082

Table of Contents

Introduction - Why You Need This Book

This book is a step-by-step guide to developing your own winning business strategy using the knowledge and brains of your own key managers. And, before you say, 'wait, they don't know enough', read on. They actually know a great deal.

What's Different about this Book?

The world is long on paper and short on action. This road tested, proven system contains everything you need to apply this strategy development process. It's built on tried and true principles and processes, and does not attempt to clutter up the field with highly sophisticated stuff that rarely has any practical application to the majority of businesses around the world. It is light on computer simulations and strong on logic. It shows you how to win. And, what's even better, it applies to virtually every kind of business.

Some parts of this book will require concentration. But, enough stories will be woven in to illustrate key points. These stories have been chosen from businesses that are unlikely to be familiar to most readers. Why you may ask? When stories from businesses with which people are familiar are used, people tend to debate the illustration in a "Well, that's really stupid! I'd do it differently" manner, rather than paying attention to the moral of the story.

Who Needs this Book?

The answer is anybody who leads or wants to lead a business, from a company with sales of a million dollars to a business with $100s of millions in sales. Here are a few specific illustrations of the hundreds of situations where this book will help you.

1 You are the head of a successful family owned business. You are approaching the age when you want to retire and do something else with your life. You also want to be around long enough that you can step in if problems develop. You need to provide clear direction for the next generation of family members who are going to take over the management or are going to serve on the board of the company. But, you need to bring the family members and the key managers along so you know that they understand how the new plan was put together, believe that it is the correct way to go, and will commit themselves to the implementation of "their" new plan. This book can show you how to get this done.

2 You are in the same situation, but you have a different problem. Over the years, you have carved off pieces of the business so that each member of the next generation has a piece to "run". This has made the company very unwieldy and there are questions as to whether all of the pieces make sense any more. You want to sort out what to keep and what to sell so that the company has clear focus and the resources necessary to build winning businesses in what is retained. This book can show you how!

3 You just got promoted to run a part of your company. Some pieces seem to fit, and others don't. You need to figure how to organize the pieces and parts so they fit into a pattern that makes sense in terms of how the market or possibly – the various markets work. How do you sort this out? This book can show you how to do this.

4 You just got handed a business that is in a real mess. It's a notorious turnaround. It's like the old De Soto division at Chrysler – any young manager who showed great promise was sent over to turn it around. Each burned out, and left the company. You don't want this to happen to you. But, you also need to bring the management team you just inherited along with you on your new journey. How do you figure out how to fix the business and get the and at the same time get the management team to join in with you? This book can show you how!

5 You work in a company that plans informally and the seat of the pants style seems to be wearing a bit thin. You want to volunteer to create a formal strategy to lift the business to a higher level. But, you need to convince your boss to let you take a swing at creating a winning strategy. This book will help you convince the boss that you know how to do it!

6 You want to enter in a new business in a new market in which your company has never competed before. Well, you're in luck. This is exactly the case study chosen to help you through the strategy development process. It is a step-by-step explanation of how you go "where you have not tread before" to paraphrase a phrase from Star Trek.

7 You run a large company with several divisions and business units operating in many countries, each with very different market conditions. You want to make certain that each significant market is being addressed properly, but you don't want to spend millions doing it. And you want country management to be deeply involved and committed to the results of the project. This book will show you how to train a team to do this quickly, efficiently and successfully.

8 You have just gotten involved with a large merger and you need to sort out and the pieces and parts. You need to decide whether the existing structures need to remain separate, or are there pieces that need to be combined into larger and more powerful wholes. The first question is 'do any of these pieces naturally fit together, or will the force fit answers end up combining apples and oranges. This book will show how to sort these questions out.

9 The chairman has just handed you a monstrous volume supposed to be a strategic plan. There is an enormous amount of data included. However, you are not certain that it

really gets to the point of what is needed to underpin a successful strategy. You can use this book as a checklist to answer your questions or find out what is missing.

There are dozens of other situations in which you can apply the strategy development process described in this book. These are just a few of them. The key to all of them however, is to follow the dictate of the market. That is the objective, neutral and most effective course to take.

What's ahead?

There are 6 chapters and appendices included in this book.

Chapter 1: Background on what makes a strategy successful and common problems that need to be overcome.

Chapter 2: Begins the case study showing how to carry out the competitive analysis that is the foundation of a winning strategy. This case analyzes how to enter a brand new (to the client) market in the early days of its growth. This is not all light-hearted recitation of amusing anecdotes. Your interest is having your business win. That is serious stuff. This is a serious book.

Chapter 3: An explanation of how to use the key strategy development tools in your work to develop a winning strategy. In covers Market Maturity which explains how to different levels of market development, Competitive Position which shows you which strengths are needed at different levels of market maturity, and when strategies work best.

Chapter 4: An analysis of the strategy choices the team working in this case study made and the plan they created around these choices.

Chapter 5: A review of what you have learned and synthesizes the key elements of the strategy development process.

Chapter 6: Describes how you can apply the process to each of the situations posed in the Introduction. This illustrates a number of approaches to adapting the process to different situations. One size does not fit all, but you can make modifications to adapt the strategy development process to work very effectively in virtually any situation.

Appendices containing all of the materials used in the development of a strategy follow Chapter 6. Also included are a number of exercises used to help explain to strategy development teams how the pieces and parts work. These are important. You may reproduce your own forms from this book for your own use.

Also included is an outline listing each of the steps in the process. You have to use judgment in working with this outline. It includes the comprehensive list of topics to be covered. Not every topic is relevant to every business. For example, you will see references in this comprehensive list to a review of past strategies. This obviously can be dispensed with when you are crafting a strategy for entry into a new market. The ones that don't fit tend to be self-evident. Use your judgment and eliminate those topics that clearly don't fit your specific situation.

Chapter 1 - What Makes a Strategy Successful

Using this process, you can develop a strategic plan for your business that is every bit as good as if you had hired a high–priced consulting firm for $100s of thousands of dollars. This book is your guide in creating a strategic plan for your business. You will learn how to build this plan with the people who work for you, and who will play a critical role in executing your new strategy successfully. But to get this done, you have to remember that this is a serious guide to a very rigorous process.

The most important thing to remember about strategic plans is that you should play to win and win where winning is worthwhile. Winners in any market reap the greatest rewards in terms of profits and satisfaction. There is a simple truism: winning is much more fun that losing. Watch any high school football game. Listen to the fans of the two teams as they leave the stadium. Those associated with the winners are happy and ebullient. Those associated with the losing team are subdued. Your team will respond wonderfully to winning.

You should focus on winning, even if it is only in a segment of the market you are examining. But the area on which you are focusing your efforts on winning should be attractive enough that you can generate significant rewards.

The approach outlined in this book is extremely economic in time and it only requires six days of working sessions with your strategy development team to create the strategic plan. In addition, you will need some off line time from those participants to complete as part tasks assigned as their part of the next steps developed at the end of work sessions 1 and 2. Consider the alternatives:

1 A seemingly endless series of half-day meetings in which it rare that a conclusion is reached. Eventually, everyone runs out of patience and one ends up with a strategy by fiat; or

2 Delegating the strategy development work to staff or to an outside firm, which means that your team will be presented with a fait accompli in which they had no hand in creating. This generally leads to dissension and negativity.

You need to emphasize to your people that developing the strategy for your business is really important. One way to demonstrate this is to hold the working sessions during the regular work week. Making everyone come in on weekends sends a powerful signal that strategy development is not important enough to do on company time.

The fundamental principals of strategy have evolved over the centuries, first in the military sphere and then in the 20th Century, the business world and government began to adapt formal strategic thinking to their somewhat unique needs.

Any discussion of the subject needs to start by defining some the underlying concepts of effective strategies. It is relatively easy to create something that resembles a strategic plan. It is very difficult to create and implement an effective one.

Let's start with some basics. No strategic plan is anything but a very expensive book unless it is implemented effectively. Any strategic plan that aims to be implemented successfully must meet 4 principles, the first three of which were formulated in the early 19th century by Karl von Clausewitz.

1 <u>Concentration of Effort</u>. This calls for the strategy to focus on the most important goal, the one that will have the greatest impact on success. - KvC

2 <u>Economy of Force</u>. True economy is achieved by committing sufficient resources up front to ENSURE success. KvC More recently, Dwight Eisenhower echoed this when he said "*Never send a battalion to take a hill if a regiment is available.*"

3 <u>Consistency in Pursuit of the Goal</u>. Continue to focus on the goal until success is achieved. Eliminate or phase out the rest. KvC "*The essence of strategy is choosing what not to do.*" — Michael E. Porter

4 <u>Understand, Believe and Commit</u>. Those individuals critical to executing the strategy "*must understand how it was developed, believe in its correctness and commit themselves to its successful execution. In our case, these people become the strategy development team*". – Peter von Braun

Taken together, these 4 principles drive strategic thinking towards identifying and then concentrating effort against the most important goal governing success, marshalling sufficient resources to ensure that success is achieved, maintaining this focus until the goal is reached, and led by a team that understands how the strategy was developed, believes in its correctness, and commits itself to executing it successfully. Strategic plans that meet these tests generally succeed.

What can lead to strategic failure? The reasons are legion, but most have to do with human mistakes.

1 <u>Doesn't Focus on Winning</u>: Winners in a marketplace earn the majority of profits. Simply "participating" in a market without a clear aim at winning is a commitment to losing. A concentration on winning provides focus to your efforts and leads to improved effectiveness. Many, many times the refrain has been heard "Well, we participate in the XYZ market and try to get our fair share". No! Figure out how to win, not participate.

2 <u>Not My Plan</u>: There is an old adage to the effect that "Strategic Plans are the way MBAs at Division communicate with MBAs at Corporate". Operating management, defined as everyone who is critical to the success of the plan, must be deeply involved in its development. They are the ones who must understand how it was put together, believe in its correctness, and commit themselves to its success. The key operating management must "own" their plan.

3 <u>Measure the World</u>: Strategic plans often are accompanied by a tremendous wealth of data, which tends to obscure both focus and clarity. For those so inclined, this can lead to endless debate that hampers progress by encouraging indecision. It's the "We still don't have a precise measurement of XYZ" syndrome. Typically, only 4 or 5 measurements turn out to be critical to the success of the plan, and many of these have

to do with competitor actions. You need to concentrate on these, and not waste time on interesting, but not vital, items.

4 <u>Insistence on Precision</u>: This error stems from the assumption that one can "audit" the future. The blunt fact is that the future is uncertain and strategic plans have to cope with that uncertainty. You should make a small number of assumptions that are critical to the success of the plan, and then monitor these assumptions to make sure that you are on track. If the assumptions change, then you may have to adapt the plan to the changing environment.

5 <u>Locked in Time</u>: This quote makes sense: *You have to be fast on your feet and adaptive or else a strategy is useless* - Charles de Gaulle. Many companies "lock down" their strategic plans for a finite period of time – say 3 to 5 years. Barring a cataclysm, the plan remains almost inviolate during that period. This leads to it becoming less relevant as the plan becomes increasingly estranged from what is happening in the world. The best solution is to adopt a "rolling" approach to strategy development. This does not mean re-writing the plan every year, but rather taking a critical look at the environment and the pace of implementation to determine if any changes of substance need to be made in the plan.

6 <u>Unrealistic Breadth</u>: Many strategic plans are overly broad and try to cover too much territory by including many businesses in the plan. Each business should have its own strategic plan. Bluntly, a business for which it is not worth developing its own specific plan should be built significantly, sold, or closed.

7 <u>Incredibly Wordy</u>: A strategic plan should not be judged by how heavy it is. Clarity of thought and logic are more important than impressive length. The reader should be able to track to logic from starting point to conclusion. A good plan for a single business can be covered in 30 to 40 pages. Generally, operating managers won't read much more than this. It is far better that they participate and learn it from the ground up.

8 <u>Who's Right, Not What's Right</u>: You as the boss have to be very careful not to suppress the information and insights of your subordinates. You want the world in which you compete to be described as it really is, not how you would like it to be. Ultimately you will make the final decision, but encourage others to contribute as the process evolves. Unless a totally stupid analysis is emerging, don't exercise your veto until you get towards the end of the plan development. In the interim, if things are getting a bit silly, all you normally need to do is to give the session a nudge in right direction by asking the right question. Also, you get the added benefit of using the working sessions as a way to see how your people think.

9 <u>Everybody Gets a Piece</u>: Altogether too often, the available resources are too few to provide every business opportunity with what is needed to win. As a result, most of the time, everybody gets a piece of the pie, not enough to win, but enough "to keep things going". This way no one has enough to get the job done and everybody loses. So, you should start with the most important opportunity, fully resource that, and if there is

anything left, move down to #2 on your list. If there is anything left, move on to the next item on the priority list until you run out of resources. Don't give everyone a little piece. Play to win by concentrating your resources against the best opportunity!

10 <u>Inside Out</u>: Most planning processes start by looking within the company and only later looking at the outside world. This means that everything tends to be described in an "Us vs. Them" context. "What do we like to do" or "What are we good at". This creates a myopic focus and dulls one's strategic senses. Remember, everybody competes with everybody else. You can't just pick out the weakest company from among the competition and decide you are going to take their business.

Getting Started

There is often a great deal of confusion between what is meant by the words "Objective" and "Goal". You need to be clear about this before you start to develop your strategy. An objective in strategic terms is something to be worked toward or striven for. It tends to be aspirational. A goal is timebound and measurable. Here's an example: The **<u>objective</u>** of a private business is to maximize long-term profit. That maximization can't be measured, nor can one define what is meant by long-term. Contrast that with a **<u>goal</u>** of "double profit over the next 5 years". Those goals are timebound and measurable. It can be tracked over the 5-year period in time to take corrective action if necessary. Both are important concepts, but serve different purposes.

An objective is a reminder of a longer-term priority, and a goal provides focus for the here and now. Don't start off with a goal on the table. Examine the market, establish the Basis of Competition, Market Maturity, Competitive Position and then figure out what is possible before you lock yourself in to a finite goal.

No strategy has a good chance of being successful unless the people who will play a key role in implementing it: (1) understand how it was developed; (2) believe in its correctness; and (3) commit themselves to its implementation. The best way of achieving this is to determine who these people are, and make them the strategy development team. These people should include 5 to 15 or so people who have direct contact with customers. Several salespeople and a few from marketing, if you have such a department, is a great starting point. Thereafter, add one or two from finance, HR, operations, R&D, and anyone else who will play a key role in implementation. In this case, more is often better. Very productive strategy development projects have been run with as many as 40 participants, but it takes the proverbial iron hand in a velvet glove to keep the session from descending into chaos. Fifteen to 20 works well.

You as CEO should observe, but not intervene unless things get completely out of hand. Remember Mistake #4, "Who's Right, Not What's Right". It very difficult for people to be open, frank, and even make mistakes if the boss in conducting the sessions. That being the case, whom do you pick as the working session leader? Probably you should choose someone senior from marketing. Whoever you pick must drive the analytical process, not simply "facilitate". Strategy Development is not an exercise in Group Think.

Without someone neutral driving the analytical process, you might as well form a circle, join hands and sing "Kumbayah".

Folk from the finance staff generally aren't comfortable with approximations. They are used to exact numbers. Generally, people from production are too inward focused, as they should be. Leadership in this case is not simply aggregating opinions, but rather forcing through the logical process, not making everyone happy. You need to end up with a tightly reasoned conclusion that reflects what it actually takes to win in the marketplace.

A frequent objection to a strategy development team is that many in this group will not have a comprehensive understanding of the entire business. This may be true for a number of individuals. However, by participating as a member of the strategy development team, they will soon gain the understanding, which will help them understand more about how to improve your business and do a better job of accomplishing this.

In over some 30 years of experience, there is yet to be a strategy development team working in an existing business of any scale that collectively does not carry around in their heads 95% of the information necessary to develop a winning strategy. These people may not understand the significance of what they know. They may not have ever put the pieces together. They think that unless they know the exact number, that the approximations they can make are not useful, and so on. These points of view are, in the immortal words of Associate Justice of the US Supreme Court, Arthur Goldberg, "Cow Pooh Pooh".

The level of information they do have is very helpful for the development of your new strategy because this strategy development process creates contexts for information, provides cross-checks, and has many other ways of calibrating approximations so that the end result is surprisingly accurate. Secondly, by gaining this understanding, they will come to know how what they do impacts on the success of other parts of the organization, and what they can do to make the business even more successful.

Use approximations.

The participants in the first working session should be told NOT to do any advance preparation and leave their data books behind. You can't imagine how much time has been wasted during sessions because someone insists on searching through 600 or so pages of data to find one number, which generally does not turn out to be that important.

How do you calibrate approximations? The basic approach to doing this when you get to the back end of the first working session, you will review all of the flip charts to identify approximations that really need to be checked for accuracy. The acid test is if a mistake in a piece of data would change any one of the critical conclusions reached, then it must be known with a relatively high degree of precision. If it will not change the conclusions, then, as they say, "it's good enough for government work". All of the data shown in the case study was gathered during the first three day working session and is an example of how productive a management team can be.

The exception to the above is when you are creating a plan to enter an unfamiliar market about which very little is known by your managers and sales people. In this case, you probably should consider hiring some outside experts to participate, or hiring a specialized consulting firm to work <u>with</u> you. However, your key people who will be involved in implementing the plan must participate, because it is they who will have to implement whatever strategy evolves from the work.

Once you have identified the members of your strategy development team, you need to outline the work plan. Generally, the first working session should be scheduled for 3 full days, at the end of which the framework for a viable strategy is established, as well as the next steps for pushing the project forward. Subsequently, a two-day working session should be scheduled some 30 days out so that in the interim, whatever next steps developed during the first session can be completed.

The second working session is designed to resolve outstanding issues, generate alternatives and determine the requirements, risks and rewards associated with them. In addition, it is designed to integrate the data, recommendations and other information developed in the inter-session period into the draft plan and to test any tentative conclusions. The final 1-day session is designed to confirm the strategy, and finalize the plan.

The easy way to record the working sessions is the keep notes as you go along on large easel charts, which you then tape on the meeting room walls. That way, people can refresh their memories simply by scanning the charts. Use drafting tape because it comes off the wall very easily. Make corrections as you go along to update the information, and reinforce the learning experience. At the end of the session, have someone transcribe the notes and distribute the copies to all participants for review. Note: comments and corrections should be offered up during the next working session, not privately.

A final rule: once someone is in the session, they should not duck out to deal with business matters. Just personal needs. People who duck in and come back a couple of hours later must be briefed on what has happened since they left, and is generally disruptive of the process. One client really protested strongly that this policy would cost thousands of dollars of sales. Strange things do happen: it turned out that the week of the first 3-day working session was the record sales week for the year. Try not to draw a conclusion as to cause and effect for this phenomenon.

Focus on the Right Target

You need to define the scope of the strategy development project correctly. This is super important and if you don't do it right, most of your work will be wasted. It involves figuring out whether you are working with one or more Strategic Business Units, or SBUs. This buzzword has been kicked around for a long time by people who really don't understand how to use the concept and nor why it is important.

A Strategic Business Unit (SBU) is a natural business. A natural business is a business 'segment' with an independent marketplace for goods or services. If the marketplace is truly independent, then one must develop a freestanding strategy for that SBU reflecting the realities of demand and competition in this marketplace. 'Averaging' or 'merging' this marketplace and the strategies for it into other SBUs will normally result in failure to achieve the goals set for any of the SBUs in this corral.

How did the SBU concept come about? A number of years ago, a strategy team was working with the appliance division of a large conglomerate. Their specific task was to develop a strategic plan for a division dealing with "major appliances under $X00." The division included dishwashers, stoves, refrigerators, washing machines, dryers, and the rest. Nothing the team did made any sense. The marketplace simply did not operate according to defining the businesses by price category, rather than by type of appliance.

Despite the wishes of top management to achieve strategic and organizational simplicity by throwing everything into the same pot, customers do NOT choose a price band and then set out to buy any appliance that happens to fall into that particular price band. Their first priority is to buy the appliance they need, such as a stove, not to buy a washing machine instead of a stove, simply because it is cheaper. They search for a stove and then try to find one that fits into their budget.

Therefore, the team had to sort out was what they were dealing with and to create a logic structure to defend their approach. They posed the following questions to themselves, specifically, whether the business segment they were examining was:

- An independent and inseparable natural business (i.e., a Strategic Business Unit) including all of its parts; or

- More than one natural business or SBU, which means that these units need to be separated when developing strategy; or

- A part of some larger SBU within the corporation, which means that the scope of the project needs to be broadened to include all of the larger SBU; or

- A functional activity (e.g., a manufacturing or research facility) that serves several SBUs and can't develop strategy without coordinating with the managers of each of the related SBUs.

The answer to this question can be established initially through the development of a set of clues (all of which must be considered) rather than any single criterion. The nature of the clues is based on conditions in the marketplace, rather than production/cost linkages (e.g., common manufacturing facilities or methods of manufacturing), technical linkages (e.g., common technology), or common distribution channels. What rules is the end use customer. They will make the final decision.

Here's a story about what it means to be blind-sided strategically because the company defined their business too narrowly. A food industry conglomerate owned a division that made frozen baked sweet goods – Danish, coffee cake, etc. Just after WWII a series of studies were done on the product category and the conclusion was that freezing results in a more consistent and a "fresher" product when compared to the typical baked product delivered fresh through the store's front door. This is due to the fact that the frozen product is distributed through chain warehouses and does not deteriorate due to age or handling. However, these conclusions may have been well known because of landmark studies done in 1947, but they were long forgotten by the 1980s.

The client staffed its marketing department with ex P&G brand managers, who were extremely well trained and very experienced. They could promptly produce all sorts of information about sales of their products by store, by pack size, by flavor, or by day of the week. They were on top of it. They calculated that they had about a 70% share of the frozen baked sweet goods market. They met frequently to try to figure out how they would react when the inevitable call came from the Department of Justice to start inquiries about their near monopoly position in the frozen baked sweet goods market.

However, something happened on the way to the market. Two companies, Entemann's and Freihofer, reinvented store door delivery of fresh baked sweet goods. Since their products never passed through a chain warehouse, our client did not count these products in their market statistics. If they did, they would have found that they had about a 7 share of the Baked Sweet Goods market (fresh and frozen), not a 70 share.

As this real life story illustrates, it is very dangerous, if not a bit arrogant, to write competitors out of the script. Don't rely on your statistics alone. Go out into the marketplace and see for yourself what is going on.

Coming back to the discussion of how to use the SBU concept to get your market accurately defined and how to avoid being strategically blindsided like the case of the Muffin Man cited above: you need to use judgment when you are trying to make a decision as to the independence of a SBU. When you find that there is doubt about the independence of an SBU, the safe choice is to treat it as part of a larger whole. This will prevent you from being blind-sided strategically. If, in the final analysis, it is not part of a larger marketplace, this will become readily apparent during subsequent strategy development work. You will find yourself saying things like "over here it works this way, but over there it works differently". The ultimate test of SBU status is whether the market(s) being considered have a single Market Maturity, Competitive Position and Basis of Competition that will emerge later in the strategy development process. If these tests are met, then a single strategy can be developed. These concepts will be covered later in this book.

However, one can't wait until the strategy is developed to come to a decision about the scope of the business for which a strategy is being developed. There are some clues that can be applied early in the game – like now – that will help you guide the effort. The clues that initially define an SBU are:

A Strategic Business Unit (SBU) is what might be referred to as a natural business. A natural business is a business 'segment' with an independent marketplace for goods or services. If the marketplace is truly independent, then one must develop a free-standing strategy for the SBU reflecting the realities of demand and competition in this marketplace.

'Averaging' or 'merging' this marketplace and the strategies for it into other SBUs will normally result in failure to achieve the objectives set for the SBU.

Therefore, correct definition of the SBU is essential to effective strategy development. The first step in strategy development is to determine whether the business segment under consideration is:

- An independent and inseparable natural business (i.e., a Strategic Business Unit); or

- More than one natural business or SBU; or

- A part of some larger SBU within the corporation,; or

- A functional activity (e.g., a manufacturing or research facility) that is a part of several SBUs and can not develop strategy without coordinating with the managers of each of the related SBUs.

The answer to this question can be established initially through the development of a set of clues (all of which must be considered) rather than any single criterion. The nature of the clues is founded on conditions in the marketplace, rather than production/cost linkages (e.g., common manufacturing facilities or methods of manufacturing), technical linkages (e.g., common technology), or common distribution channels.

Judgment is then applied to the determination of SBU status. When there is doubt as to the independence of a SBU, the safe choice is to treat it as part of a larger whole. This will prevent being blind-sided strategically. If, in the final analysis, it is not part of a larger marketplace, this will become readily apparent during subsequent strategy development. The ultimate test of SBU status is whether the market(s) being considered have a single Market Maturity, Competitive Position and Basis of Competition for which a single strategy can be developed.

The clues, which initially define an SBU, are:

1. Prices: Do price changes on any product within the business unit necessitate price changes on:

- All other products/services;

- Only on some other products/services;

- On products in other business units?

If all other products/services are affected, then the unit is probably one SBU. If only some products/services are affected, then this provides a clue that there are probably two or more SBUs within the unit. If the product pricing in another unit is affected, then the unit under consideration is probably part of another, or larger SBU.

2. Customers: Likewise, if the unit has a single set of customers, it is a single SBU. If it has multiple sets of customers, it may comprise more than one SBU. If it shares customers with another unit, it may be part of a SBU in that unit or a larger SBU.

3. Competitors: If the unit has a single set of competitors, it will tend to be a single SBU. If it competes against distinctly different sets of companies for different parts of its customer/industry spectrum, it may be more than one SBU.

4. Quality/Style: If a quality or styling change for any product necessitates a corresponding change in other products/services, then all these products/services will tend to be part of the same natural business. If product/service quality or styling changes have no impact on other products/services within the unit, then the unit is probably made up of more than one SBU.

5. Substitutability: If the products/services sold by the unit are substitutable, one for the other, this tends to indicate a single SBU. Other such substitutable products/services marketed by other units within the corporation would also tend to be in the same SBU.

6. Divestment or Liquidation: The most nebulous, but sometimes the most revealing, clue to test for SBU status is the impact that selling or dropping the product/service has on the marketing or selling effectiveness of the remaining products/services. If divestment or liquidation has some impact, then there are at least two SBUs within the unit. If the product pricing in another unit is affected, then the unit under consideration is probably part of another, or larger, SBU.

The preponderance of evidence and clear-cut impacts are what is important in this analysis. Let's take the original example – appliances and consider refrigerators and stoves and go down the list of clues and see which are related and which are independent.

Clue	Refrigerators	Stoves
Pricing	Independent	Independent
Customers	Generally the same, but often at different times for different products	Generally the same, but often at different times for different products
Competitors	Mixed	Mixed
Quality & Style	Independent	Independent
Substitutability	Independent	Independent
Divestment or Liquidation	Independent	Independent

Given this set of judgments, one would go ahead and treat the Stove and Refrigerator businesses as separate SBUs for strategy development purposes. This should have no impact on organization structure. For example, as a result of this analysis, one would not set up a separate sales force for each product, nor would one create different distribution systems. However, it would have a significant impact in terms of how to beat competition in each of these businesses.

The next section of the book provides you with a real-life example of developing a strategy to enter the mutual fund market in another country. We call the country Potential Land. The example used is from a few years ago, and the facts, while correct at the time, but are now out of date. Therefore, it is an example that has the virtue of reality, but is not compromising any client's interests. Because it is taken from real life, the pieces fit together better than if one tried to create an imaginary strategy for an imaginary business. Also, there are some strange characteristics of the market that will make you shake your head in amazement. They are true: you can't make this stuff up. Further, businesses have been chosen that will be unfamiliar to most readers. That way, readers can focus their attention on the process and not get distracted because they believe they know the illustrated business and, therefore, quarrel with the analysis. Remember, we are talking about tracking through the strategy development process, not anything else.

The strategic framework for market entry is similar to what you would attempt to create during your first working session. This set of notes is similar in scope and detail to what you would aim to create during your first 3-day working session.

If some of the numbers concerning market size and growth seem very high, they are. But, tracking this market over the last 20 years or so, it actually happened and a company that followed this strategy would have won really, really BIG. As we work our way through the chapters, the full text of the notes will be reproduced. In addition, there will be a few text boxes that outline the material to be covered in a section, as well as text boxes that explain the significance of what has been described.

Chapter 2 - Entering the Mutual Fund Business

These are the actual notes from the first working session and document the first round work done by the strategy development team that met for 4 days to develop a strategic framework for entering the mutual funds business in Potential Land, a name selected to protect the innocent. The first few pages summarizes the briefing to the strategy development team members distributed with the notes.

Overview

This strategic framework summarizes the project and further development of a more detailed business plan. It focuses on developing a winning position, rather than simply to enter and "participate". Overwhelmingly, the bulk of the profits go to the winners, not the "hobbyists".

We recognize that there may be errors of fact in these notes contained. One of the next steps is to identify and correct these. The real value of having a strategic framework is to give the team the ability to:

- Identify the issues that will have a significant impact on the basic strategic direction of the new venture.

- Drive the analysis forward within the strategic framework and focus these analyses efficiently on the most important issues relating to the success or failure of the enterprise, rather than attempting to "measure the world".

- Develop a detailed understanding of the strategy and a commitment to its successful implementation.

- Create a detailed "roll out program".

Summary of Tentative Conclusions

Scale:

The mutual fund industry in Potential Land is forecast to grow from its estimated base of $70 billion in 1994 to $500 billion in 2000 and to $1.5 trillion in 2005. Therefore:

- A winning position will require significant scale against the forecast size of the industry.

- Scale will also be required to afford "leader level" expenditures and still achieve significant profits:

- Marketing costs, such as advertising, direct marketing and promotion, must be comparatively large (relative to competition) get above the noise level.

- Systems investment will be large and must be spread across a relatively large base.

- Given the large and growing number of public companies in which a mutual fund might invest, research requirements will be significant.

- In short, large size will be required to achieve economies of scale and earn an attractive return.

Customer Service:

Customer service may offer the most significant opportunity to achieve leadership against the Basis of Competition (described later in these notes). Currently, customer service can only be described as ranging from poor to terrible, e.g.:

- Poor liquidity

- Shareholder redemptions at large discounts (20% to 40%) from Net Asset Value (NAV), particularly in closed end funds (as an illustration, if your fund shares have a market value of $1,000, the redemption value could be as little as $600. This does not please a customer.

- Non-standard calculation of NAV (this will change as a result of a mandate from the Securities Exchange Board of Potential Land (SEBPL).

Note: The actual growth of the mutual fund market in Potential Land has been close to 30% annually. The dollar value is lower because the local currently has depreciated to approximately to approximately 20% of the US $ value in the base year of 1994.

While the government is seriously upset about this situation, policy pronouncements alone will not solve this problem. Terrible customer service is an area where particularly a new entrant can achieve significant competitive advantage. This is because it is much easier to do it right the first time than to correct the existing antiquated and inefficient systems, many of which are manual. The technology necessary for excellent customer service is available on the international market and from potential foreign collaborators.

Providing outstanding customer service also will require substantial investments in process technology, because manual systems will not be able to provide the required service quickly or economically. Integrated systems will be required for other functions, such as portfolio management, back office operations and trading as well.

Ease of Entry:

The market is relatively open, and should expand rapidly enough to allow an aggressive, capable and well-focused new entrant to build a winning position.

Next Steps

Each participant should review these notes against the following criteria:

- Does the logic hold? It is more important at this stage to make certain that we are thinking clearly than to dot every "i" and cross every "t". There is no way in which we can measure to future accurately enough to perform an accounting audit. The validity of any strategy directed at the future is essentially based on a complex series of experienced-based judgments, corroborated by such facts as are available. Therefore, we must make certain that our reasoning is sound and the assumptions we have made are valid.

- Have we correctly evaluated the competitors in the market in terms of their basic strengths and weaknesses, both qualitatively and quantitatively?

- Have we correctly determined the Basis of Competition in terms of what really drives the market? If the Basis of Competition is correct, it is unlikely that we will make serious strategic errors in our subsequent work.

- Have we correctly defined the market in terms of key customer segments and what motivates their purchasing behavior? Clearly, we must develop a deeper understanding of this purchasing behavior to guide our subsequent actions, both in terms of product development and designing the key elements of the company.

- Have we correctly estimated the basic forces driving the development of equity markets in Potential Land over the next five years and has this growth been quantified in a reasonable way?

- Does each participant clearly understand the next steps and what must be done to complete them? Are there any important steps that have been omitted? When these steps are completed, will we be in a position to finalize the plan and develop a detailed implementation program for launching the business?

- Are there any errors of fact or substance? Even the best work can be discredited by misspellings, numbers which don't tie together or other details, all of which may have little to do with the substance of the work, but make it look shoddy. Help, please!

Please remember that this is a first draft and needs substantial checking. Just because it may be neatly typed does not mean that the facts and conclusions are necessarily all correct. Please review it critically. The team will meet again in about a month at a date and place to be determined. Please hold your comments and corrections until then so that we can integrate the changes as a group and assess their strategic impact. However, if you don't understand your assignments, please speak now rather than go down a blind alley.

Scope of Strategy Development Project

All types of mutual funds in Potential Land.

The Mutual Funds Industry in Potential Land competes for assets against a broad group of financial services, including asset management, primary and secondary stock market operations, savings institutions and corporate fixed deposits. However, structural and market development effects exercise a major influence over the impact of this competition, for example:

- High Net Worth Individuals have the broadest range of investment options, and generally have not favored mutual funds.

- Corporations generally have not broadly participated in mutual funds.

- Middle class, retail investors have limited access to other forms of stock market investment and the Government of Potential Land tends to encourage mutual funds as an appropriate investment vehicle for these customers.

Market Size and Growth

Currently, Mutual Funds control only a small proportion - around 3% - of financial assets, $70 billion of an unidentified total of about $2.1 trillion (excludes bond market, the team needs to get these figures and add them to the following table).

Investment Form	$ Billion	Number of Competitors	Number of Competitors Controlling 80% of Market
Primary Stock Market (New Issues)	30	5,000	100
Secondary Stock Market	450	18	2
Bond Market including Government	0		
Closed End Funds	50	130	2
Open End Funds	20	3	1
Savings (often in Gold kept at home)	1,800	75	5
Company Fixed Deposits	10	8,000	N/A
Asset Managers	1	N/A	N/A
Total	2,361		

Note: Total does not double count mutual funds.

Growth

Growth in the equity market, and of the mutual fund industry, which participates in it, are estimated below:

Category	$ Billions			
	1990	1994	2000	2005
Equity Market	50	450		
Open End Funds	3	20		
Closed End Funds	7	50		
Total Mutual Funds	10	70	500	1,500
Number of Public Companies	300	700	1,500	3,000

Key Influences on Growth

Key Influences on Growth is an attempt to explain the factors that are driving the market up or down – sometimes conflicting trends ending up going in both directions. An assessment of these factors allows you to get a "Kentucky Windage" readings on the future of the market. Doing this can also suggest new product opportunities, such as eliminating particular ingredients, or modifying the functions performed. It is worth spending considerable time on this because it can be very helpful in predicting the future.

Key Influences On Growth

- Liberalization - abolition of CCI (Controller of Credit Issues)

- Growth in personal income among upper/middle class

- Privatization increases the number of large company equity issues

- Growth of company profits

- New investors entering the market

- Foreign money (Non Resident Potential Lands, Multinational Corporations, Foreign Institutional Investors)

- More institutional investors within Potential Land

- Improved Information

- Infrastructure development, particularly technology-based communications

- New products in terms of market perception - open ended funds, new instruments

- Conversion of debt to equity, corporate restructuring

- Abolition of wealth tax, decrease on corporate and individual tax rates

- Liberalization of withholding increasing the amount of money available for investment

Limitations on Growth

- Stock market infrastructure - depository and settlement, spreads

- Lack of access to primary/secondary market on retail level.

- Lack of effective regulation.

- Primitive corporate communication

- Weak research

- No "GAAP" or common standard of accounting principles applied to company financial statements.

- Poor distribution

- High transaction costs - 1% brokerage / custody 0.7% / Stamp tax 0.5%

- Very high spreads

- Theft, fraudulent shares

- National, computer-based trading system - supposed to be online April 1995

- Bombay Stock Exchange scheduled to go on computer in June 1995 (real 1996)

- Drop in trading costs could be significant

- The new entrant company should start with interconnect capability.

Competition

Government deregulation and encouragement of the mutual fund industry has led to a doubling of competitors since 1990.

Increase in Number of Mutual Fund Companies	
1990	1994
10 (public)	19 (9 new, all private)

However, market share positions, while changing, are still highly concentrated, reflecting decades of Government "supervision" of the market and sponsorship of Government-owned companies.

	$ Billion		Market Share	
	1990	1994	1990	1994
UTI	?	50	90%*	70%
Can Bank	?	5	?	7%
State Bank of Potential Land	?	4	?	6%
General Insurance Corporation	?	1	?	1%
Morgan Stanley	0	1	0	1%
Subtotal	?	61	100%	85%
14 other companies	?	9	?	15%
Total	?	70	?	100%

* 100% in 1988.

Competitive Analysis and its Role in Strategy Development

Competitive analysis is one of the most important elements of the strategy development process, and in many cases, it is the most important part. The end process of the competitive analysis is the development of the Basis of Competition based on the analysis of those competitors that are winning and why. The Basis of Competition defines which company is most likely to win in the marketplace. It also identifies the improvement steps your company will have to take to become the winner.

The Basis of Competition also serves as the most useful guide to day-to-day decision-making. If an action strengthens a company against the Basis of Competition, it probably is a good idea. If the idea does not demonstrably strengthen the company against the Basis of Competition, then it is probably not a good idea. Every employee should concentrate their efforts on those actions that strengthen your company against the Basis of Competition.

The steps in the Competitive Analysis section are as follow:

1 Competition:

a   Number of competitors - increasing or decreasing?

b   Names and market shares of current major competitors (quantified to the extent possible).

c   How is the leader's share changing - relative to the SBU?

d   Industry stability - entrants versus failures.

e   Foreign competition (size and growth).

2 How important is this industry or industry segment to the SBU's competitors (e.g., relative profitability, emotional commitment)?

3 Organizational nature of competition (free standing company or division).

4 Degree of integration, forward or backward (e.g., leaders are integrated from raw material to final product).

5 Competitor strengths and weaknesses, and strategic thrust as perceived in the marketplace.

6 Degree of integration, both forward and backward

7 Product line concept and unique values offered (specialty/commodity matrix).

8 Barriers to Entry

A cautionary note: It does not happen often, but some times a unit in one of the geographical divisions of a large company will try to rig the data in their favor. This happened during a world-wide review of its seed business for another multi-national company. We worked with the management of the larger country units to develop their individual strategies. You might think that, for example, corn is corn is corn and one size would fit all.

Not so. Take one dimension. In the U.S., the predominant use of corn was animal feed, to which now the manufacture of ethanol has been added, consuming some 40% of total corn crop. In Mexico, the major use is for human consumption. In South Africa, the major use is for beer (for which sorghum is used as well). It should be no surprise that these different uses are met with quite different corn varieties. Using one variety to serve the different end uses would be as though one tried to serve the motor vehicle market with an all-purpose vehicle to be used as a family car, fire engine and city bus. Wouldn't work. Each seed variety must reflect its end use and is not interchangeable.

One European country, presented a rather strange phenomenon. The market was described as being substantially larger than one would have suspected. We work on approximations, which are generally good enough for developing a strategic framework. But the initial profile was just downright silly. The client's market share appeared to be significantly larger than indicated by the casual briefing back at HQ had suggested. Like by a factor of 10X.

What had happened is that the client's unit sales volume in that country had been reported in "quintiles", which equals 1/10th of a ton. All the competitor's data was reported in tons. That explained the 10:1 discrepancy in sales volume. Second, this division claimed that the only road to success was to develop a family of "Departmental Hybrids". They said that each geographic Department, of which there were 480, had its own unique micro-climate. Seeds that worked in one, would not work effectively in any other. Each

Department had its own agricultural inspector, and unless the specific seed variety was to be endorsed by the local inspector, the local farmers would not adopt it.

How did this happen, you might ask? The leadership of this division had asked the divisions that had gone through the process earlier and then cooked up their answers, and then drilled the staff in the "right" answers.

It didn't take too long to determine that the two leading competitors, with shares of 25% and 35% respectively, offered just two to three varieties each. A new entrant built the 25% share position with superior products in just 5 years.

So what's the take away? This process has too many cross-checks for someone to try to "rig" the answers. But, you as the leader of the strategy development process have to be alert for stuff that sounds funny. Generally, markets are logical constructs. It may take a little time to figure out what their individual logic system is, but once deduced, logic generally rules.

Foreign Competition

A number of foreign companies have entered the mutual fund market in Potential Land, all but one with an Potential Land collaborator.

Foreign Company	On Own	With Potential Land Collaborator	Name of Collaborator
Morgan Stanley	XXX		
George Soros		XXX	General Insurance
Kemper		XXX	20th Century
Pioneer		XXX	Kothari
Daiwo		XXX	CRB
Lazard Brothers		XXX	Credit Capital
Kleinwort Benson		XXX	Tata
Morgan Grenfell		XXX	Arvind Mills-Anagram
Guiness		XXX	First Leasi
Capital Guardian		XXX	Birla

Importance of Industry to Competitors and Structure

Company	Importance	Structure & Comment
Unit Trust of Potential Land	High	Independent, almost 100% of business
State Bank of Potential Land	High	Division, 50% of company net profit
Morgan Stanley	High	Independent, must solve huge problems
Soros/GIC	High	JV, 33% Soros
Lazard/Credit Capital	High	JV, other JVs with Lazard
CanBank	High	Division, importance because of problems
Pioneer/Kothari	High	JV, Pioneer weak
Apple Finance	High	Division
ICICI	High	Division of excellent development bank
Morgan Grenfell/Arvind	High	JV, start-up
Guiness/First Leasi	High	JV, start-up
Kemper/20th Century	Medium	JV, Kemper transfers technology
Capital Guardian/Birla	Medium	JV, Start-up
Life Insurance Corp.	Medium	Division
IndBank	Medium	Division
Bank of Potential Land	Medium	Division
Punjab National Bank	Medium	Division, very regional
JM	Medium	Division of merchant bank, broker
Daiwo/CRB	Low	JV, Daiwo nominal partner
Kleinwort Benson/Tata	Low	JV, Tata "hobby", start-up

The reason that the business is of high importance to so many competitors is the large current size, roughly $70 billion in 1994, and the massive future size and growth rate predicted for 2005 of approximately $1.5 trillion at the 1994 exchange rate.

Competitor Strengths & Weaknesses
Note on Evaluating Competitor Strengths & Weaknesses

You need to exercise discretion in judging strengths and weaknesses. There is an all-to-human tendency to demonize any action a competitor can take that you can't do because your company's policy prevents you from using. A wonderful example of this came up during a strategy project for a multi-national client doing business in Argentina. The normal distribution channel for this product was through farm stores in various parts of the farm country. Obviously, if the client's products were not on display in the farm stores during the period leading up to planting season, the likelihood of their being sold decreased significantly. And, given the long restocking cycle, once sold out, then it would take some time to re-supply the farm stores.

Surprisingly when the 2 or 3 leading competitors were roundly criticized as using "unethical sales practices". The members of the strategy development team were adamant "what our competitors do is absolutely wrong. And, there is nothing we can do about what they are doing". And, several members of the team were vitriolic about the perfidy of their competitors. This was a first in terms of this kind of condemnation of a competitor.

After probing this charge very carefully, and expecting to find something absolutely awful – kidnapping the farm dealers' kids, or some such evil. No, these competitors sold their goods to the farm dealers on consignment. The dealer did not have to pay for the competitor's products until the farm dealer had sold them on to the farmers. Being able to buy on consignment created significant incentives for the farm dealers to stock more of that company's products. And with more stock on the floor, the competitors were much more likely to outsell the client. Why was this practice branded as "unethical"? Well, the multi-national parent company did not want its divisions to sell on consignment because they were worried about a possible credit risk. As it turned out, there was no record of a credit risk stemming from these consignment sales.

What's the lesson to be drawn from this story? If what you hear sounds a bit strange, probe behind the statement. Don't be satisfied until you understand the reasoning behind the statements. Yes, one could be convinced that competitors selling on consignment placed the client at a significant disadvantage. But, that practice was not against the law, and rather than being an unethical practice on the part of its competitors, it revealed a real weakness on the part of the client.

Note on Evaluating Competitor Strengths & Weaknesses (Cont'd.)

A competitor will be rated as having a "Strength" factor if is ranks in the top 10% to 15% of all of the competitors being rated. Likewise to have a weakness, it must be in the bottom 10% to 15% on that factor. Anywhere in between is neither a strength nor a weakness.

In addition to strengths and weaknesses, you should also try to capture the general characteristics and apparent strategic thrust of each competitor. In some cases, the apparent strategic thrust can simply be "being there". This is particularly true in markets where one or more leading competitors is government sponsored and has had a virtual monopoly for a significant period of time.

Competitor Strengths & Weaknesses

UNIT TRUST OF POTENTIAL LAND

General Characteristics & Strategic Thrust
- 30 years old, oldest company in the mutual fund business in Potential Land
- Concentrated focus
- "National" company
- Government owned
- $50 billion under management

Strengths
- All Potential Land reach; offices throughout the country
- 900,000 collection agents
- All offices linked by computer for after sales service
- Regarded as a high performer
- Regarded as providing high safety
- 70% share
- Leverage on the buy side
- Best trained Asset Management staff
- Career path for employees
- Broadest product line, in market all the time
- First choice for investors
- Promoted by owner (Government of Potential Land)
- Superb infrastructure relative to competition
- Can offer loans - gets good deals on conversion

Weaknesses
- Government uses UTI as a prop for the market
- Pressured to buy shares of Government companies
- Government dictates some portfolio structure
- New rules prevent adjusting performance of individual funds through interfund asset transfers (ability to do this may be ending)
- Poor customer service (driving restructuring project)
- Shares of open ended funds NOT redeemed at NAV minus 20%
- Largely closed end funds (Assets 67% closed / 33% open)
- Terrible Custody
- Commingled assets (Securities Exchange Board of Potential Land now requires segregating assets
- 12 qualifications on balance sheet
- Unreconciled physical inventory of securities documents (5%)
- Often delivers the wrong certificates
- As oldest and biggest player, has the largest inventory shortfall exposure

STATE BANK OF POTENTIAL LAND

General Characteristics and Strategic Thrust
- Owned by SBPL
- Autonomous Division
- $4 billion under management
- Started 1984 - 2nd oldest
- Considered to be major profit contributor - 50% of Bank's 1994 net profits

Strengths
- Considered / is one of the 3 largest mutual fund organizations
- Bank viewed as capable, MF also, Bank Officers run MF
- Branches (10,000 throughout Potential Land) generate 25% of funds
- Viewed as safe
- Good performance (1 of 3 top)
- Customer service centers linked on-line
- Strong research, market perceives banking position strengthens research
- Excellent knowledge of Government policy, interest rates
- Widely consulted by Government, industry
- Bank gives position to launch many new types of funds - FOREX, etc.
- Ability to trade internally, lowers transaction losses

Weaknesses
- Too many tiers of decision making (true for all government sponsored funds except UTI – the best managing directors & top managers left during the past 3 years)
- High turnover of fund managers
- Sent back to bank after 5 years
- Raided by competitors
- Government / Bank pay scales (10 - 20% of private mutual funds)
- Fund managers also perform all administrative functions

KEMPER/ 20TH CENTURY

<u>General Characteristics and Strategic Thrust</u>
- 20th Century was one of the first, now is the leading non-bank finance company, founded by 4 Citibank people
- $20 million net worth
- Manages $100 million in mutual funds
- Mostly private investors
- Only $5-10 million in public funds
- Tie-up with Kemper to get technology and brand name to support future growth

<u>Strengths</u>
- Strong corporate relationships
- High profile promoters
- CEO respected by Potential Land corporate powers (old business houses)
- Research advantaged by parent relationships and knowledge
- Finance skills aids MF management (how?)
- Aggressive

<u>Weaknesses</u>
- Bad market timing - launched right after Morgan Stanley debacle
- Autocratic, hands-on-style

MORGAN STANLEY

General Characteristics & Strategic Thrust
- Leveraged the US-Potential Land country fund; MS set this up with the State Bank of Potential Land
- Launched the Potential Land/Potential Land fund on own
- Only independent foreign mutual fund company
- Positioned itself as the Gold Standard
- Independent, did not form a joint company with a Potential Land company, and restricts its collaboration to the individual fund level.

Strengths
- High cost / high quality portfolio management
- Highest profile foreign name (foreign names often thought to be good)
- Good customer service in technical terms
- Established self as "respected foreigner" through marketing - though this image is now lost due to scandal
- Established reputation for high quality / high presence research
- Strong political connections
- Star system built around manager (works in Potential Land)

Weaknesses
- Viewed as cheats and incompetent
- Promoted shares as IPO
- Allowed a gray market to develop through brokers affecting around 5% of shareholders (offering price was 10 / sold to some customers at 30)
- Suspicion management skimmed the premium
- After issue closed, bid price dropped to 7 from 10 at the offering
- Still below par (market index 100, MS 80, NAV 9.8)
- Performance below market - threat to reputation
- Market waiting for year end statement and portfolio - April
- Launch caused large scandal
- Most existing shareholders probably would not invest with MS again

SOROS / GIC

General Characteristics & Strategic Thrust
- True JV
- Managed by Soros now
- Viewed as conservative
- Strategy - began with bringing foreign funds to Potential Land ($600 million invested at NAV), then launched Potential Land funds
- Autonomous
- General Insurance Corporation has a monopoly on non-life insurance business
- Manages a total $1.15 billion

Strengths
- Launched open end fund
- Viewed as conservative
- Soros has a great name
- Uses GIC's insurance agents for distribution (1 million)
- 10 customer service centers
- Broad product line
- Strong technology - on-line to service centers
- Good portfolio management
- Excellent performance against - market /promises
- Offers discounts on insurance (5% - 35%)
- Open end - weekly valuation

Weaknesses
- Seen as Government company and having constraints on fund managers
- Government pay scales re very low, creating a real retention problem
- Low profile - market doesn't recognize funds good performance

LAZARD BROTHERS / CREDIT CAPITAL

General Characteristics & Strategic Thrust
- $200 -300 million under management
- 25% from Foreign Companies & IFC / 5% Potential Land (Where is the rest?)
- (Please include a short description of Credit Capital and their types of business)

Strengths
- Able to tap Potential Land & Foreign Institutional Investors FII)
- Strong retail, ethnic-based position in the West

Weaknesses
- Small
- Poor performance
- One man show, NOT an organization
- Tied broker - suspected of skimming or front running

CANBANK

General Characteristics & Strategic Thrust
- 2nd largest State Bank
- Identified with South Potential Land
- Originally operated in South Potential Land, now a national company
- Grew quickly to $4 billion under management around 1991, no growth since then because of Government of Potential Land restrictions
- Essentially static, closed for new business

Strengths
- Used to be aggressive, now restricted by government because of scandals & operating weaknesses
- 2nd largest mutual funds company
- Used to be able to make quick decisions with devolved authority

Weaknesses
- Lost assets, lost ability to recover assets - Crane scandal implicated CanBank and former CanBank people
- SEBPL restricted new schemes for
- Demoralized staff (seniors made juniors take the blame)
- Poor performance against market
- Now bureaucratized
- Poor public image
- Tied purchases (past)
- Suspect integrity

PIONEER/KOTHARI

General Characteristics & Strategic Thrust
* Manages $350 million
* $123 million came directly from Reliance, $2 million from public for the 1st issue
* 1st Private fund, flopped in market because market was not ready
* 2nd Fund got public response

Strengths
* Very good client service - prompt delivery / fast redemptions, although this capability has not been tested against the mass market
* Aggressive, capable marketers
* First profits class technology (please be specific)
* 100% annual gain, super performance, which is real
* First to offer frequent NAV announcements
* Excellent research
* "Parent" Reliance is a major player in M & A and corporate development
* Pioneer gets first call

Weaknesses
* Narrow customer base, but growing

APPLE FINANCE

<u>General Characteristics & Strategic Thrust</u>
- Manages $50 million
- Launched in mid-1994
- Parent company is only 10 years old
- Parent company started in computer software training and finance (merchant banking, car finance)
- Built $150 million net worth in very short time
- Opportunistic

<u>Strengths</u>
- Skilled in capital markets
- Rapid decision-making
- Aggressive, involved top management

<u>Weaknesses</u>
- Mutual fund has low profile
- Weak asset management
- Company has no focus, not winners in any of their businesses (float what's "hot")

Integration

In some businesses being integrated backward to raw materials sources (as in the petroleum industry) or forward into the distribution or retail systems, can be a tremendous competitive advantage. In the case of the mutual fund industry in Potential Land at the time of this project, the situation was as follows:

*   No significant integration, forward or backward

*   Only two companies have broker connections

Product Line Concept

The majority of the funds offered are equity funds. However, there have been tax incentive-based funds offered in the past. Due to changes in Government of Potential Land regulations and legislation, these funds will not be offered in the future. Some fixed income funds are offered, but these are not greatly differentiated. Sector funds are just emerging, with two examples being funds that invest in power-related securities and Export Oriented Units (EOU).

The chart below compares these products on a specialty/commodity matrix. However, Potential Land mutual fund pricing is not driven by specialty / commodity issues to any great degree as yet. As the market matures, greater pricing freedom may emerge at the specialty level.

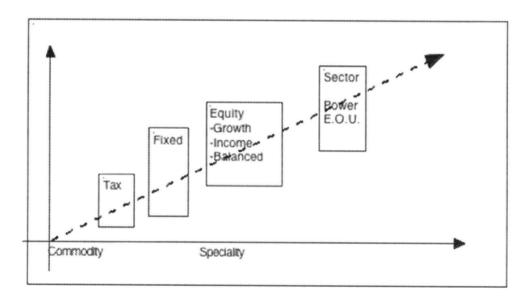

Barriers to Entry

Obtain License from Securities Exchange Board of Potential Land (SEBI)
*   Prove credentials (identity of sponsors is a key factor)

- Demonstrate net worth of $50 million in contributed capital; substantial substance of sponsors implying back-up helps a great deal

- Five years experience in the financial sector

- Tie in with, or ownership of, a well respected name

- Shortage of skilled and trained personnel

BASIS OF COMPETITION

It has been emphasized that you should set "Winning" as your business objective. And, you should aim to win in a market or large segment of the market where winning will generate substantial returns. Your motto should be "Play to Win and Win Where Winning is Worthwhile".

You will note that we haven't evaluated the client company as of yet. This is done on purpose. It is an attempt to get a perspective on the business from the market's point of view. In developing the Basis of Competition, focus on the winners in the market and determine what are the factors that cause customers to choose to do business with them.

Simplistically, one can fall back on the old standby: "price, quality, service". However, one has to qualify each of these factors. In order to make this work, you need to dig behind the overall categories. For example, one of the three factors cited can conflict with others. Quality needs to be defined carefully along several dimensions. Differences in quality need to be easily recognized by consumers along a dimension they care about. The cost of obtaining that aspect of quality needs to be low enough that it doesn't force you into a price level that is above what consumers are willing to pay.

When you examine the Basis of Competition shown in a few pages, several things jump out:

1 Investor confidence based on the sponsorship of the company. In a new market, particularly one aimed and managing a substantial part of a family's assets, the question of who stands behind the product is of primary importance. Hence, investor confidence leaps to the forefront.

2 Portfolio performance. How well does the company manage my money? One can't predict future performance, but most people think that the past is a good predictor of the future.

3 Fair price. Notice the word "fair". This was crucial, because customers were not as concerned about the management fee as they would be in the U.S. Given the tremendous differences in how Net Asset Value and redemption price were calculated by some of the competitors, these items became a very important part of the total price an investor would pay. Redemption prices can be discounted by as much as 25% or more (yes, really!) from the value of the assets in a customer's account.

4 Customer service. The factors explaining what is meant by customer service are listed underneath this item on the Basis of Competition and explain what is meant in this market.

Another useful caveat when developing the Basis of Competition, generally speaking if the winners aren't doing it, it probably isn't important, unless you can reasonably forecast some sort of a "revolution" in customer behavior, or a really serious unmet need.

Therefore, it makes all kinds of sense to figure out what it will take to win. The easy way of doing this is to figure out what today's winners are doing. And the key to doing this is to determine what today's Basis of Competition is. This is the place to start. Even if you have figured out a wonderful technological advance that will improve performance significantly, the improvement has to be along a dimension that the market values.

You will note that we haven't evaluated the client company as of yet. This is done on purpose. You need to get a perspective on the business from the market's point of view. In developing the Basis of Competition, we want to focus on the winners in the market and determine what are the factors that cause customers to choose to do business with them.

Simplistically, one can fall back on the old standby: "price, quality, service". However, one has to qualify each of these factors. In order to make this work, you need to dig behind the overall categories. For example, one of the three factors cited can conflict with others. Quality needs to be defined carefully along several dimensions. Differences in quality need to be easily recognized by consumers along a dimension they care about. The cost of obtaining that aspect of quality needs to be low enough that it doesn't force you into a price level that is above what consumers are willing to pay.

When you examine the Basis of Competition, several things jump off the page:

1 Investor confidence based on the sponsorship of the company. In the new market that has developed around mutual funds, particularly because it is aimed and managing a substantial part of a family's assets, the question of who stands behind the product is of primary importance. Hence, investor confidence leaps to the forefront on the Basis of Competition.

2 Portfolio performance. How well does the company manage my money? You can't predict future performance, but most people think that the past is a good predictor of the future. If nothing else, it gives a buyer confidence that the management team has won in the past, and has a reasonable chance to win again in the future.

3 Fair price. Notice the word "fair", not "lowest" price This was crucial, because customers were not as concerned about the management fee as they would be in the U.S. Given the tremendous differences in how Net Asset Value and redemption price were calculated by some of the competitors, these items became a very important part of the total price an investor would pay. Redemption prices could be discounted by as much as 25% (yes, really!) from the value of the assets in a customer's account. That means that a difference of 0.25% in price could be only 1% of the redemption discount from NAV. Which would you choose? A difference of 0.25 percentage points in the annual charge, or losing 25% of the value of your assets when you redeemed your fund?

4 Customer service. The factors explaining what is meant by customer service are listed below and explain what Customer Service means in this market.

- Transparency

- Prompt redemption, and payment of dividends

- Prompt delivery of share certificates, transfers, etc.

- Communications

- Disclosure

- Market updates

- Results

- Account information

- Dial in data

- Grievance resolution

- Convenience

In addition to honesty and fair dealing, customer service in this case making the customer a part of the operation of the fund by allowing access to information, both about his account and about what is going on in the market. This can result in many more questions about what is going on, but dealing with the customer in this manner breeds far more loyalty than ignoring their needs to know what is going on.

When developing the Basis of Competition, this is the level of detail that is necessary. You must be able to define fairly precisely how the factor operates and what it really means. Therefore, you can't fall back on the old trilogy of "Price Quality, Service". Therefore, don't try to short cut this part of the strategy development process. Debate it, thrash it out until you are convinced that you have nailed the Basis of Competition correctly. Another useful caveat, generally speaking if the winners aren't doing it, it probably isn't important, unless you can fairly forecast some sort of a "revolution" in customer behavior, or a really serious unmet need.

BASIS OF COMPETITION

Do not <u>wish</u> failure on your competition. <u>Plan It</u>.

The following represent the Basis of Competition, the "rules" which govern Winning in the marketplace for mutual funds in Potential Land:

- Investor confidence based on:

- Sponsorship of the company, typically through a joint venture with a credible foregin partner

- Perceived quality of management

- Portfolio performance

- Past record

- Research

- Fair price

- Redemption spread

- Calculation of Net Asset Value

- Customer service

- Transparency

- Prompt redemption, and payment of dividends

- Prompt delivery of share certificates, transfers, etc.

- Communications

- Disclosure

- Market updates

- Results

- Account information

- **Dial in data**

- **Grievance resolution**

- **Convenience**

The Basis of Competition not only defines which company has the highest likelihood of winning in the marketplace, but it also serves as the most useful guide to day-to-day decision making. If an action strengthens a company against the Basis of Competition, it probably is a good idea. If the idea does not demonstrably strengthen the company against the basis of competition, then it is probably not a good idea.

Moreover, for a new entrant, the Basis of Competition is a compelling list of what you should be trying to build.

Normal Distribution Channels

Channels	Customers	Assets	Comments
Brokers	20%	40 %	High Net worth Individuals
Agents	80%	60%	Largely SBI, UTI, GIC, all of which are government companies
Direct	0	0	

Seasonality

There is not any significant seasonality, although seasonality used to be a significant factor when tax-oriented funds were offered.

Role of Technology

Current role is **Low**

The future role of technology in Potential Land will focus on process technology already generally available in the U.S., concentrating on:

Client Service and Account Management

- Computerized Portfolio Management

- Calculation of NAV / Repurchase price and redemption process

- Client Reporting - telephone, on line and customer communication

- Marketing support

<u>Administration</u>
- Loss control and inventory management

- Trading and order execution

- Depository

<u>Research</u>
- Database

- Portfolio simulation

Financial Operating Characteristics

<u>Operating Costs</u>

The profit economics of the mutual fund business are highly leveraged on fixed costs, as shown in the illustration of the operating costs of a typical mutual fund company below:

	$ Millions		$ Millions		$ Millions	
Customers	200,000		2,000,000		5,000,000	
Assets / Customer	$1,000		$1,000		$1,000	
Costs for customer account (transaction, custody, etc. up to 3% of assets)						
Assets under Management	200		2,000		5,000	
Revenue	2.25		20.0		50.0	
Company Costs		Trans-fer*		Trans-fer*		Trans-fer*
Office Space	0.5	0	1.0	0	1.8	0
Portfolio Managers	0.4	0	1.0	0	2.5	0
Senior Admin.	0.5	0	0.5	0	1.0	0
Support	0.1	0	0.2	0	0.4	0
Marketing	1.3	1.0	2.0	1.5	3.0	2.3
Research	0.5	0	2.0	0	3.0	0
Client Service	0.6	0.5	6.0	5.0	15.0	12.0
Computer Ops.	0.2	0.1	0.8	0.4	1.5	0.8
Benefits	0.7	0	1.2	0	3.0	0
Total Operating	4.8		14.7		31.2	
Transfer to Customer		1.6		6.9		15.1
Net Operating	3.2		7.8			
Profit Contribution	-1.0		12.0		33.9	
Contribution %	-44%		60%		68%	

* Costs allowed to be transferred to the customer's account.

Step back for a moment and consider why a company would want to enter the mutual fund business in Potential Land. If successful, a new entrant would be risking $12.6 million to start a business that at the industry average performance could generate between $12 million and $34 million annually, which if it grew at the same rate at which the market was predicted to grow, over 30% annually compounded, then the future value of the earnings would be in the range of $400 million. So, maybe the future value of the earnings would only be 25% of that. Still very worthwhile. The business model is there and working. What is needed is to find a foreign partner with the reputation and the systems to provide the missing elements.

Financial Operating Characteristics (Cont'd.)

Start-Up Costs

Note: This analysis was done for raising $200 million in the first 6 months, it needs to be revised for a target of $500 million.

Item	$ Millions		
	Total	**Exposure**	**Fronted**
Statutory Capital	5.0	5.0	5.0
Start-up expenses			
Advertising	4.0	4.0	2.0
Promotion and PR	0.1	0	0
Brokerage (3.5%)	7.0	0	0
Registrar (1%)	0.4	0	0
Lead Manager fee (0.5%)	1.0	0	0
Subtotal	12.5	4.0	2.0
Charged against assets	12.0		
Net Cost	0.5	0.5	0.5
Staff and preparation	1.2	1.2	1.2
Legal & Accounting	0.1	0.1	0.1
Computer	1.0	0.5	1.0
Systems	1.0	1.0	1.0
Other	0.3	0.3	0.3
Subtotal	3.6	3.6	3.6
Total	9.1	12.6	10.6

Price Trends

Standard fees today:
- Management fee of 1.25% below $10 Million in total fund assets, 1% above $10 million in total assets committed to funds

- All competitors charge full fees

- Market is performance sensitive, not fee sensitive, although this could be changing

- However, attention focuses on redemption discounts from Net Asset Value, which range from 20% to 40%. These discounts are much, much more important than the level of fees charged for account management.

- Improving redemption discounts will have far more impact on customers than fee discounting and is the major way of improving consumer benefit

Sales Terms
- 100% payment is required with application

Customers
- 300 million Potential Lands in middle class - increasing at 5% to 10% per year

- 40 million Potential Land citizens have Purchasing Power Parity incomes of US $30,000 or more

- Customer categories:

Category	Number	% $ in MF	Buy Open End	Comment
Corporate	1,000	15-20%	Yes	
HNWI ($1 million in Financial Assets)	100,000	5%	Yes	Normally not buyers of Mutual Funds
Urban	25 mm	67-75%	Yes	1 million in 1980
Rural	500,000	5%		

Purchasing Behavior
- Only about 15 - 25% of Potential Landers who own shares have purchased mutual funds

- Government is actively supporting mutual funds as means of providing middle class with access to securities markets

- Investment in securities (as opposed to savings instruments and property) is a relatively new phenomenon

- Population has a high savings proclivity (20%+ of annual income)

- Investing (in the past and still today) is felt to be speculative, not conservative

- Customer must have full amount of mutual fund purchase in hand and in cash

- Low liquidity due to prevalence of closed end funds and high discounts from Net Asset Value

- Discount from NAV for closed end funds used to be 40% and within the last six months has dropped to 25% to 35%

- Lack of access to both the securities markets and to financial information, although the latter is now improving

Demographics/Psychographics
Corporations
- Bought as treasury instrument on short-term basis

- Major buyers of money market funds

High Net Worth Individuals (HNWI)
- Some investment through asset managers (slight), most participate in the stock market directly, property and money lending

- HNWI are a mixture of business owners (predominant group), professionals, landowners, entertainers, etc.

Urban Middle Class
- Salaried (55% of MF investors now are government employees, 65% have a professional qualification)

- Disposable financial assets in $20,000 to $50,000 range

- High future personal financial obligations for family housing purchase, marriage expenses for children, professional education

- Typically relatively young (just married and saving) or over 45 with children settled

- Goal-oriented investors – saving / investing for a purpose

- Financial objective is an inflation-adjusted, positive rate of return with little risk of loss of capital

Age Group	% of MF Assets	Comment
Under 30	25%	Married, earn 2 salaries, save a significant portion of one salary
30 - 45/50	25%	Normally no new additions
50+	50%	Add significant new money

- Major barrier: no "monthly" investment programs - the normal pattern has been to subscribe in full to new closed end fund

- Open end funds have limited additional purchase options

At this point, we have described the market thoroughly, and it is time to begin the analysis of our own company, which we have designated the **Pot of Gold JV** as its preliminary project name - acronym = POG

Pot of Gold JV – General Description

- Start-up seeking foreign partner to gain technology, credibility, and experience

- Launch product to be an open end, frequent additional purchase equity product

- No legal constraint on producing this type of product

- Administrative constraint prevents fractional shares

- New application with each purchase is required, but process can be simplified and automated

- Constraints should be able to be overcome

- HNWI product offering

- High liquidity

- Linked lending facility with participating bank

- "IPO" fund

- Short maturity closed end fund (2 - 4 years) to reduce discount with rollover option

- Corporate Product

- "Money market" open end fund

- Low/no spread on Net Asset Value for higher end investor

- Portfolio mix 80% equities, 20% bank overnight call market for liquidity

Building Strengths in the JV
- Foreign Partner with significant reputation

- Own funds invested will represented 10% of investment pool in fund

- Customer Service - best in industry

- High Performance

- NRI Fund

- US-Potential Land Fund

- Technology acquired from US will be on par with best in Potential Land

- Publicizable history

- Build "Star" system / brand by recruiting top Potential Land fund managers

- Financial strength

Weaknesses
- Unknown in Potential Land mutual fund market

- as finance company

- as top 10 company

- as a strong consumer franchise in the financial services industry

- Startup

- "Why You ?" - skepticism about the appropriateness of ACL's entry into the mutual fund business, despite long history of success in other fields

Chapter 3 - Key Strategy Development Tools

The tools used in this strategy development process are meant to focus thinking and save a great deal of work and debate. As with almost any human process, if it drags on too long, your people will lose interest, they will forget what lead them to a conclusion, and they will begin to ignore what is happening around them. This is clearly not a good thing. Hence, speed is an essential in driving towards a successful conclusion.

This section of the book deals with three very important tools that normally mesh together logically and will save you a great deal of work and time in developing a Winning Strategy. But, that is what they are – tools wrought by man, and therefore, fallible. All of the tools don't fit every single circumstance. In the 40 years or so that this system has evolved, it has been rare to run across a situation where they have not fit well. Most of the time when they haven't fit perfectly, it is because we haven't figured out something about the way the market really operates. Once we have figured this out, then everything works just fine.

For example, while working on a project to develop a strategy for the hybrid corn business in Mexico (another market with which most of you may not be familiar!), the first cut at the Basis of Competition just did not make sense. The winners included a company (the government seed company) that charged higher prices, and one whose seeds did not perform as well. It just didn't make sense.

Part of it did. The government seed company (poorer performing seeds) would extend "crop terms" – the farmer could get an interest free loan for his seed from a local agricultural credit agency which did not have to be paid until after the harvest was in. No quarrel about why the government seed company offering interest free loans to poor farmers sold a lot of seed. Only a very few companies could offer these terms, but each company had to be on the list of the ones "approved" in Mexico City. But, there was one semi-approved company that sold a great deal of seed along the northern border districts.

What was their secret? They rented a fleet of flat bed trucks and refrigerated vans. Each flat bed truck was set up as a stage. When they came into a farm town large enough to have an agricultural credit office, they would set up the stage on the back of the truck. Go-Go dancers from Texas would perform and cold beer was passed out. Then the local farmers were invited to go talk with the folks in the Agricultural Credit office and induce them to add the sponsoring company to the list of approved seed vendors. Worked like a charm for a number of years. This did not show up on our list of the original factors comprising the Basis of Competition

The tools explained in the following section are:

• Market Maturity

• Competitive Position

• Periodicity of Strategy Application (try saying that 10 times very fast)

Market Maturity

Market Maturity represents the major factors that determine the dynamics at work in a specific market. The chart on the next page depicts the factors that operate during a specific dimension of market maturity. These change significantly as a market matures. Unlike biological maturity, market maturity can reverse itself, something that scientists of every dimension have been seeking since the origin of the Fountain of Youth myth.

First of all, there are 4 broad stages of Market Maturity – Embryonic, Growth, Mature and Aging. Let's examine one of the descriptors used in assessing Market Maturity – the Growth Rate of the Market. In the Embryonic phase, percent growth in 100's and is accelerating. Remember, this can mean sales increased from 10 units to 100 in the 2nd year. Typically, a meaningful rate can't be calculated because the base is too small and changing so rapidly.

In the Growth phase, the annual rate of increase is in 10's, as in 50%, 30% or so, but is constant or decelerating. In the Mature phase, market growth is in single digit. And often is cyclical, particularly in later stage growth markets. In fact, cyclicality is a convincing signal that the market has matured and that demand is subject to outside influences, such as the state of the overall economy. In the aging phase, industry volume cycles but declines over long term. As volume declines, competitors drop out of the market, leading to the "last dynamite factory" effect. When there is only one supplier, prices can rise and the business can become quite profitable as long as demand continues. It becomes a market governed by "profits for one, disaster for two".

The most important aspect of Market Maturity is the impact it has on corporate actions. Actions taken prematurely or too late can lead to disaster. The case of Texas Instruments foray into electronic watches is a case in point. In the early days of the market, LED technology ruled the roost. TI decided to get a jump on the market and built a large manufacturing facility dedicated to LED technology. Unfortunately, just as the factory, with production lines dedicated to LED technology was completed, the technology shifted to LCD, which used far less power and featured extended battery life. Competitors who had hung back and waited for the technology to "mature" were rewarded and TI lost a great deal of money by being the first to leap into large scale production facilities to automate and drive down costs.

The take away: Market Maturity is a very, very important concept and plays an important role in determine a company's strategic choices. The chart on the following page illustrates the way the market typically evolves against the 7 key determinates.

	Market Maturity Guide			
Descriptor	*Embryonic*	*Growth*	*Mature*	*Aging*
Growth Rate	Percent growth in 100's; accelerating; meaningful rate can not be calculated	Percent growth in 10's; but constant or decelerating	Single digit growth; cyclical	Industry volume cycles by declines over long term
Industry Potential	Usually difficult to determine	Substantially exceeds Industry volume, but is subject to unforeseen developments	Well-known, primary markets approach saturation volume	Saturation is reached; no potential remains
Product Line Breadth	Basic Product line is established	Rapid proliferation as product lines are extended	Product turnover, but little or no change in breadth	Shrinking
Participants	Increasingly rapidly	Increasing to peak; followed by shakeout and consolidation	Stable	Declines; but business may break up into small co's.
Share Distribution	Volatile	A few firms have major shares; minor shares are unlikely to gain major shares	Firms with major shares are entrenched.	Concentration increases; or shares are dispersed to locals
Customer Loyalty	Little or none.	Some; buyers are aggressive.	Suppliers are well-known; buying patterns established.	Strong; number of alternatives decreases.
Ease of Entry	Usually easy, but opportunity may not be apparent.	Usually easy; the presence of competitors offset by vigorous growth.	Difficult; competitors are entrenched, and growth is slowing.	Difficult, little incentive.
Technology	Concept development and product engineering.	Product line refinement and extension.	Process and materials refinement; new product line development to renew growth.	Role is minimal.

Market Maturity (Cont'd.)

These dynamics have a major impact on the type of strategy likely to be successful for this business. The interplay between Market Maturity and the selected strategy is a key determinant in defining the risk profile for the strategy chosen for the business under examination.

MARKET CHARACTERISTIC	Stage of Development			
	Embry-onic	Growth	Mature	Aging
Growth Rate		X		
Industry Potential	X			
Product Line Breadth	X			
Number of Participants	X			
Share Distribution	X			
Customer Loyalty		X		
Ease of Entry		X		
Role of Technology		X*		
Overall	X	X		

* Process technology requirement to provide customer service

The reasoning behind the evaluation of Market Maturity for the Potential Land mutual funds market is summarized below:

Growth Rate:

The market is rated as being at the early stage of Growth, which means that it should grow very rapidly - perhaps 30% to 50% per year, perhaps very unevenly.

Industry Potential:

The potential of the industry is substantial - and in this case, factorially exceeding current industry volume. However, it will be subject to unforeseeable developments.

Product Line Breadth:

The basic product line has been established in the marketplace and product proliferation of product types is just beginning. There is likely to be a great deal of product experimentation during the period of rapid growth. Not all of these products will be successful, but the experimentation will be a necessary part of establishing which of the various product offering the market will find attractive.

Number of Participants:

This factor is rated as late Embryonic, or possibly early growth. There will be a large number of new entrants. Sometime in the relatively near future, there will be a considerable shake-out as the "hobbyists" and some of the new entrants will fall by the wayside during the period of consolidation as the market enters the late Growth stage. Therefore, it will be critically important to achieve scale early and build a substantial position of strength in the marketplace.

Share Distribution:

Share distribution is rated as volatile. Substantial share positions can be built during this stage of market development. Later, as the market enters the later Growth stages, companies with minor shares will be unlikely to acquire major shares. Well-focused and well-managed, aggressive development should be well rewarded at the current stage of market development.

Customer Loyalty:

This factor is rated as early Growth. There are peculiarities in the Potential Land market, but there are also some key characteristics. The emphasis placed on the identity of the sponsors and other factors of similar nature indicates that few, if any, mutual fund companies have established a solid reputation on their own. Moreover, it appears that most of the current product/service offerings do not meet the requirements of substantial numbers of Potential Land current and potential investors. Identifying and meeting these unmet demands most likely will be rewarded in the marketplace.

Ease of Entry:

This factor has been re-rated early Growth. Entry is usually easy because the presence of competitors is offset by the vigorous growth of the underlying market. An anomaly is represented by the presence of an established company with an enormous current market share - UTPL. However, UTPL's position may well be analogous to IBM's position 10 years ago: an enormous reputation and position based on a technology about to become obsolete.

Role of Technology:

This factor is rated late Growth, as the emphasis will shift rapidly to process technology. Because Potential Land investors will have relatively small accounts, and customer service is so important in terms of building market share, most of the technological emphasis should be on process technology - performing the service and administrative tasks in a very cost-effective and efficient manner. Without this capability, the ability to provide service at all will be jeopardized, let alone being able to do it economically.

COMPETITIVE POSITION

Competitive Position is directly linked to Market Maturity. The internal strengths a company must have to be successful change as the market it serves moves through the various stages of development. For example, embryonic markets are ill defined and often very fast moving. Companies that will be successful in an Embryonic market must have management and an organization that respond very quickly to changes in the external environment. Companies competing in mature or aging markets normally do not need this capability because the technology is almost a commodity (one can buy a complete plant from someone exiting the business, for example); product lines are well-established; brands are strongly established customers have developed significantly loyalty towards one or another company/ brand/ or product. Since the markets don't change very rapidly, management has plenty of time to carefully consider, study and temporize.

Correspondingly in mature markets, companies normally do not have to take large risks because most elements of market behavior are well defined. These enterprises evolve managements and organizations that are bureaucratic and risk-averse. They may be capable of taking risks because of their accumulated financial strength, but their managerial systems rarely reward executives who take risks. Very often risk taking is penalized. Conversely, such a system would kill a business operating in an embryonic market.

A very important point is that there is no "preferred" level of Market Maturity. The most important thing is that your company match what it does and its strategy to the level of maturity in which its market finds itself. Companies are not the measure of maturity, MARKETS ARE. Remember, the market rules, you are the one that needs to adapt to what it demands.

The evaluation of Competitive Position combines the Basis of Competition specific to a particular market - in this case mutual funds in Potential Land - and the generic factors inherent to the stage of Market Maturity of the market in which the business is engaged.

These generic factors applying to a particular stage of Market Maturity are described in the first exhibit following this page. The second exhibit evaluates POG's Competitive Position as of the point of market entry and assumes that it has done an adequate job of preparing for market entry. The system rates the significant competitors against POG in terms of whether they are better than, equal to, or worse than POG on each factor. Since one competes against all competitors, not just the weak ones, the most important ratings are the ones against the strongest players.

Different factors apply to each level of Market Maturity used in analyzing Competitive Position. Where these factors apply is summarized on the Chart on the following page.

Competitive Position Rating System

	Embry-onic	Growth	Mature	Aging
1. To be strong on the Basis of Competition				
2. To have high share in your market				
3. To have an increasing market share				
4. To be gaining more points of share than the leader				
5. To be one of three companies with leading shares				
6. To have a protected market position, e.g. patents, etc.	****			
7. To have price leadership in your market				
8. To have a broad product line for your market				
9. To have a strong corporate and/or brand name		****		
10. To be free from dependence on few customers		****		
11. To have total costs that are low relative to competition		****		
12. To have lower variable manufacturing costs per unit				
13. To have sufficient volume to support optimal distribution				
14. To be operating at close to optimum capacity				
15. To have special relationships with other entities				
16. To have profitable alternatives for your production facilities				
17. To have production facilities larger than viable new units				
18. To have profitable operations				
19. To be producing a net cash flow				
20. To have as much forward integration as competitors				
21. To have as much backward integration as competitors				
22. To have a strong technology relative to competition				
23. To be capable of taking risks because of overall strength				
24. To have a managerial system supportive of risk taking				
25. To be able to quickly respond to external changes		****		
26. To have a business that is unattractive to competitors				

The actual ranking of Competitive Position rates each of the competitors against your company. The rating is very simple: is the competitor better, the same as or worse than your company. The ranking factors include the Basis of Competition, as well as all of the generic factors which apply based on the maturity of your specific market is shown below for **POG.**

Competitive Position Rating System Definitions

Ranking Factor #1 – To Be Strong on the Basis of Competition

Being strong on the Basis of Competition is the most important factor in the Competitive Position Ranking System. If you are very strong on this factor, you have a significant chance of winning. If you are not, get there or get out of the business if the market is Mid Growth to Aging phases. This factor cuts across all levels of Market Maturity.

Ranking Factor #2 - To have high share in your market

Other than by using a high degree of linguistic legerdemain, there is no way you can be a Winner if you do not have a high share of the market in which you are competing. This factor applies across all levels of Market Maturity.

Ranking Factor #3 - To have an increasing market share

This is a common mistake in thinking about Competitive Position. The winner could have a 60% share and holding steady at that level. You could have doubled you share by going from 1% to 2%. You're still not the winner. If you are taking significant share points each year from the leaders, it is reasonable that you should get a plus on this factor.

Ranking Factor #4 - To be gaining more points of share than the leader

Basically, the same logic as that for #3 holds – you could have gone from 1% to 2%, thereby doubling your share, while the winner could be static at 60%. There is no way you can be the winner at a 2% share.

Ranking Factor #5 - To be one of three companies with leading shares

Absolutely necessary to be one of three leading companies in terms of market share. As in 1 and 2 above, cuts across all levels of Market Maturity

Ranking Factor #6 - To have a protected market position, e.g. patents, etc

If this factor plays at all, it plays in embryonic, before the market fully develops. Generally speaking, by the time the market enters the growth phase, there are multiple ways to achieve whichever product attributes that are important and, with the exception of patented pharmaceuticals and a few other research-intensive products, the markets are generally fairly open.

Ranking Factor #7 - To have price leadership in your market

Price leadership, if it plays at all, is applicable during the Mature phase of a market, when production methods have standardized to the point that price, not performance becomes a major differentiator. The price leader typically has the power to force other competitors to follow it's lead.

Ranking Factor #8 - To have a broad product line for your market

This factor becomes important during the Growth Phase of a market, when it has not standardized on the few product variations for which demand is the greatest and the market is still in search mode. When it matures, several things happen: the leader has a relatively narrow product line limited to the high volume products, and the trailing companies are stuck with the low volume, and therefore, expensive products.

Ranking Factor #9 - To have a strong corporate and/or brand name

This factor can play in Growth, and does play in Mature and Aging, by which new strong names could have become established. When one looks at many of the new categories of consumer electronic products, the leading players are new companies. For example, IBM dropped out of the personal computer market.

Ranking Factor #10 - To be free from dependence on few customers

This factor is strongly influenced by the art of the possible. In embryonic, one may only have one customer. As the market moves into its growth phase, the number of customers will expand. If one does not have a broad customer base in Mature, your company is in trouble. By the time the market enters Aging, you are stuck with whoever is still a customer in a shrinking market.

Ranking Factor #11 - To have total costs that are low relative to competition

This is a very important concept. It is TOTAL COSTS that matter. There have been many times working with large multi-nationals that because of the application of their superior manufacturing technology have low costs at the local level, but by the time that several levels of overhead get layered on, their cost structure is no longer competitive. However, this is a factor that becomes important when the market becomes price competitive, typically during Mature stage of Market Maturity.

Ranking Factor #12 - To have lower variable manufacturing costs per unit

This is the corollary of number 11 above. Having lower variable manufacturing costs per unit is helpful, but it is total cost that counts.

Ranking Factor #13 - To have sufficient volume to support optimal distribution

Plays in the Growth and Mature phases when price competition begins to become the norm and therefore, effective management of costs becomes important. Also, you need to be able to cover the bulk of the market efficiently.

Ranking Factor #14 - To be operating at close to optimum capacity

This says very little about your company's position in the market. It speaks to your production capacity, which could have no relation to what the market needs or could buy.

Ranking Factor #15 - To have special relationships with other entities*

This factor, while often prized by company management, is normally illusory. Unless it is something that grants almost monopoly power, which could create problem with regulators, it means you are dependent on an external entity, which could come to dominate you. Not a source of strength for you.

Ranking Factor #16 - To have profitable alternatives for your production facilities

Why would you think that this is a source of strength? If you have profitable alternatives for your production facilities, why aren't you serving that market?

Ranking Factor #17 – To have production facilities larger than viable new units

This is only a source of strength during the early to mid phases of Growth because you can grow significantly without adding capacity, leverage fixed costs, and only have to concerned about variable costs. Presumably as you use more of the existing capacity, your margins should improve significantly.

Ranking Factor #18 – To have profitable operations

This plays significantly during the Growth, Mature and Aging phases of Market Maturity. During the ramp up phase in Embryonic, it is unlikely that your operation will be profitable form an accounting standpoint.

Ranking Factor #19 – To be producing a net cash flow

This is vital during Mature and Aging. It is generally not possible as you are investing in product development in Embryonic, nor during Growth, when the market is expanding and you are investing everything you can get your hands to support that growth.

Ranking Factor #20 – To have as much forward integration as competitors

This is a function of stability in the marketplace and finding the right scale. Buying up retail distribution is an example. Done prematurely, it is very easy to get the scale wrong and you end up with too much or too little of a good thing. If you have too little, you end up competing with your non-owned retailers, who will soon drop you. This operates during Mature and Aging.

Ranking Factor #21 – To have as much backward integration as competitors

Backward integration means moving down the distribution change towards your sources of raw materials or component manufacturing. During Mature, it can often allow you to achieve lower costs, but in Aging, it can mean that you have more capital tied up in capacity that you can't use.

Ranking Factor #22 – To have a strong technology relative to competition

Absolutely necessary during all phases of Market Maturity. The technology shifts from product technology, applicable during Embryonic and though to mid-Growth, to production technology from late Growth through to Aging, when the role of technology shifts to "make it faster, better, cheaper". However, it could be argued that there is effectively no role of technology in an Ageing market because you can buy up anything you need from those who have gone out of the business, and because the market is shrinking, it is unlikely anyone will invest in new technology.

Ranking Factor #23 – To be capable of taking risks because of overall strength

Capability to take risk does not mean that there is a willingness to take intelligent risks. Until the recent madness hit, large insurance companies were classic example of institutions that certainly had the capacity to take risk, but rarely if ever did so. This factor plays an important role in Embryonic and Growth, because these are the phases of Market Maturity during which risks frequently need to be taken. In contrast, companies competing in Mature markets typically have a well developed bureaucracy. They can afford to be ponderous because the market does not change very rapidly, so they can study, assess and procrastinate without danger.

Ranking Factor #24 – To have a managerial system supportive of risk taking

Applies during Embryonic and Growth. Useless unless it is combined with the capability to take risk. However, absent this factor, as described above, the willing to take risks is not very useful unless the company has the resources necessary to do so.

Ranking Factor #25 – To be able to quickly respond to external changes

Applies during Embryonic and Growth. These are phases of Market Maturity during which one can go home on Friday and when one comes back in on Monday, the world has changed. By late Growth, the market has calmed down a bit and possessing this capability is less vital to success.

Ranking Factor #26 – If it is unattractive to your competitors, why is it attractive to you? One could argue that this is a variant of the "protected position" concept, essentially it says that you are protected because you are in a really lousy business. Find something better to do with your time and your capital.

Definitions:
+ = Better Than; O = Same as; ▼ = Worse than

FACTORS	Competitors								
Competitors	#1	#2	#3	#4	#5	#6	#7	#8	Fix
Confidence - Sponsor - Management	+	+	▼	+	O	▼	▼	+	+
Performance - Past - Research	+	+	▼	+	+	▼	▼	+	
Customer service:									
- Transparency	▼	▼	O	▼	▼	▼	▼	▼	
- Redemption	▼	▼	▼	O	▼	▼	▼	O	
- Delivery	▼	O	O	O	O	▼	▼	O	
- Communications	▼	▼	O	O	▼	▼	▼	O	
- Grievance	▼	▼	▼	▼	▼	▼	▼	▼	
- Convenience	+	+	▼	+	▼	▼	O	▼	
High Share	+	+	+	+	+	O	+	+	+
One of Three	+	+	O	O	O	O	+	O	
Broad Line	+	+	▼	+	O	▼	▼	O	+
Brand	+	+	▼	+	▼	▼	▼	O	+
Distribution	+ +	+ +	▼	+ +	O	+	+	▼	+
Profitable	+	+	+	+	▼	+	+	▼	+
Strong Tech	▼	▼	▼	▼	▼	▼	▼	O	
Capable of Risk	+	+	+	+	▼	▼	▼	+	
Willing to Risk	+	+	+	+	▼	▼	▼	+	
Quick Response	+	+	▼	+	▼	▼	▼	+	+
Current Position	+7	+8	-6	+9	-8	-11	-9	+1	
3 Years from Launch	0	+1	-13	+2	-15	-18	-16	-6	+7

Well, you might say: why are there fewer competitors on this table than examined earlier in this report? There simply is not enough space for that chart in this book. The next question is "How do we interpret this visually complicated chart?" First of all, the vertical axis represents factors from the Basis of Competition down through Customer Service – Convenience. Then the generic factors from the relevant level of Market Maturity as listed on the chart titled "Competitive Position Rating System" shown a couple of pages back. The combination is what is relevant to the Mutual Fund business in Potential Land.

Your Guide to the Future

A key feature of the chart is the vertical column titled "Fix". This column identifies the areas in which POG could improve enough over the first three years to have a real opportunity to upgrade its Competitive Position. Obviously, these opportunities must become part of the strategy and its implementation plan.

The second line from the bottom, labeled Current Position" is also critical. This calculates the value of all of the factor ratings, positive, negative and neutral to determine the current position. In this case, if POG has been accurate in forecasting what its initial position will be, it will be at a strong competitive disadvantage to the 3 leading competitors, about at parity with 1 competitor, and should be clearly superior to 4 others that have been really taking advantage of their customers.

The bottom row, labeled "3 years from launch" summarizes the competitive factors that could be engaged in POG's favor with hard work and some luck. This row shows the significant improvement in POG's Competitive Position if it can pull this work off. Three years out, if successful, POG should be at parity with 3 leading competitors, should be advantaged against 2 competitors, and superior to 3 competitors.

All of this assumes that none of the other companies do not improve their competitive position by acting on their own, and that no new competitors enter the market. Those are pretty big assumptions, but you have to start somewhere, and life is a continuum of constant improvement.

Strategy

Similarly, Strategic Choice is related to the Basis of Competition, Market Maturity and Competitive Position. Different strategies normally operate better, or are more likely to succeed, at different stages of Market Maturity. But first, let's list the alternative strategies

Alternative Strategies	
A. Initial Market Development	M. Excess Capacity
B. Market Penetration	N. Market Rationalization
C. Maintenance / Same Product, Same Market	O. Distribution Rationalization
D. Same Product/New Market	P. Product Line Rationalization
E. New Product/Same Market	Q. Production Rationalization
F. New Product/New Market	R. Technological Efficiency
G. Backward Integration	S. Methods & Functions Efficiency
H. Forward Integration	T. Traditional Cost Cutting
I. Export Same Product	U. Hesitation
J. Licensing Abroad	V. Little Jewel
K. Development of Overseas Facilities	W. Pure Survival
L. Development of Overseas Business	X. Unit Abandonment

And as you might expect, the period during which a strategy generally makes sense to employ is strong influenced by Market Maturity, as illustrated by the chart on the next page. That chart shows when a strategy generally will be successful, it correctly executed in light of the Basis of Competition and backed by sufficient resources. The left hand edge of the shading indicates the beginning of the period of applicability of the strategy, and the right hand edge of the shading indicates the stage of Market Maturity at which the strategy can normally be expected to loose its efficacy.

Natural Period of Strategy Execution

	Embryonic	Growth	Mature	Aging
A. Initial Market Development	xxxxxxx	xxxxx		
B. Market Penetration	xxxxxx	xxxxx		
C. Same Product/Same Market		xxxx	xxxxxx	xxxx
D. Same Product/New Market	xxxx	xxxxxxx	xxxx	
E. New Product/Same Market		xxxx	xxxx	
F. New Product/New Market			xxxxxx	
G. Backward Integration		xx	xxxxxx	
H. Forward Integration			xxxxxx	
I. Export Same Product		xxxxx	xxxx	
J. Licensing Abroad	xxxx	xxxxx		
K. Development of Overseas Facilities		xxxxx	xxxxxx	
L. Development of Overseas Business		xxxx	xxxx	
M. Excess Capacity		xxxxx		
N. Market Rationalization		xxxx	xxxxxx	
O. Distribution Rationalization		xxxx	xxxxxx	
P. Product Line Rationalization		xxxxx	xxxxxx	
Q. Production Rationalization			xxxxxx	xxxxxx
R. Technological Efficiency		xxxxx	xxxxxx	
S. Methods & Functions			xxxxxx	xxxxxx
T. Traditional Cost Cutting			xxxxxx	xxxxxx
U. Hesitation			xxxxxx	xxxxxx
V. Little Jewel			xxxxxx	xxxxxx
W. Pure Survival				xxxxxx
X. Unit Abandonment	xxxxxx			xxxxxx

Now lets return to our case study and see what the team picked as their favored strategies. In addition, there are notes outlining what the team wants to achieve with each strategy.

Chapter 4 - Strategy Development Team's Choices

<u>Goal</u>: Achieve 3% market share by 1999
<u>Strategy</u>:

Primary Strategy - Initial Market Development

To invest in creating a primary demand for a product new to a large number of customers

A significant number of Potential Land investors have never purchased a mutual fund. Efforts will be made to understand the reasons for this, and given favorable economics. The focus will be on:

- Develop channels and approaches to reach these customers

- Stress the dual requirements of marketing communications - educate and persuade

- Determine if special products are required, and if so, design products for these customers

- Customer service standards designed to be the most cost-effective and user-friendly in the industry

- Pricing, e.g., reducing spreads against NAV wherever possible

- Products tailored to the requirements of specific customer segments

Support Strategies
Market Penetration

To increase market share through manipulation of the marketing mix,; e.g., lower price, product line breadth, increased product and sales service, increased advertising

In this case, the primary emphasis will be on:
- Customer service standards designed to be the most cost-effective and user-friendly in the industry

- Pricing, e.g., reducing spreads against NAV wherever possible

- Products tailored to the requirements of specific customer segments

Technological Efficiency

To improve operating efficiency through technological improvements in physical plant, systems and processes

Technological inefficiency results in a significant number of the areas of consumer friction between the mutual fund management company and its customers, as well as causing significantly higher costs than the international model. Therefore, POG shall strive to address these problems through such things as:

- Using appropriate "off-the-shelf" software systems, probably acquired overseas

- Making every effort to computerize its operations from the beginning in order to reduce long-term costs, support customer and avoid being overwhelmed by success

- Using technology to improve the effectiveness of customer service and communications

Methods & Functions Efficiency

To invest in new ways of doing existing task by adding new "soft" technology, e.g., new patterns of work flow, computer-aided processing, so as to improve effectiveness and efficiency

State-owned institutions have established the patterns for mutual fund company operations. POG shall devote considerable effort to such things as:

- Critically examining established patterns of organizing workflow to identify lower cost approaches to delivering superior service

- Determining if it is possible to fundamentally restructure the nature of the work done, most particularly in not using the computer to mindlessly automate useless tasks, or tasks which can be restructured to capture the benefits of the new platform.

Key Assumptions

Gloriosky! The team has now picked the Primary Strategy and the Support Strategies needed to set the direction for their plan. One of the items mentioned early in the book was that while you cannot measure the future, nor accurately predict it 100% of the time, you can monitor it effectively. You do this by making assumptions about the future that are key to the success of the winning strategy you are developing.

The ones the Strategy Development Team put together as the background for the strategy we are now going to establish for entering the mutual fund business in Potential Land are listed below:

1 Economy
- National Growth - GDP - 5-6% - This critical because it will enable the growth of capital to support investment in the mutual fund industry

- Corporate profile - 30-40% of corporate excess funds will be invested in mutual funds, particularly as liquidity improves and the redemption percent relative to Net Asset Value of the customers' accounts reaches international standards

- Government Influence – continued emphasis on

- Deregulation

- Privatization

- Free Market

- Government will continue to promote mutual funds

- Competitive Climate

- The market will become more competitive as the market becomes more sophisticated and competition increases to focus on the fair treatment of customers along the lines laid out in the Basis of Competition

- Easy Entry if one has capital and credibility

- Foreign Companies will continue to play a major role, especially for new entrants needing to bolster their appeal to customers

2 Mutual Fund Industry
- Growth – The market will grow from $70 billion in 1994, to $500 billion in 2000, and on to $1.5 trillion in 2005

- Stability - stable, some withdrawals, more new entrants

- Competitor Actions - Aggressive

- Potential Threats

- Breakdown of infrastructure (custody)

- Cyclical downturn in market

3 Market
- Price Trends - No deterioration in fees because higher redemption pay out against NAV has far greater impact

- Cost Trends – costs will decrease because of improved technology and economies of scale

4 Influences on market
- Labor climate should improve

- Social Trends - investment in securities becoming more popular in comparison to gold

5 Market Maturity - remain early to mid- growth

Financial Projections

All Mutual Fund Assets (1994 = 70,000)	ALL FIGURES IN $ MILLIONS				
	98,000	140,000	190,000	270,000	380,000
	1995	**1996**	**1997**	**1998**	**1999**
Previous Year Assets	0	500	1,800	4,065	7,565
New Assets	500	1,000	1,500	2,000	3,200
Growth of Base Assets		150	540	1,200	2,300
Growth of New Assets		150	225	300	500
Total Assets	500	1,800	4,065	7,565	13,565
Revenue	5	18	41	76	136
Cost of Operations					
Portfolio Management	0.8	1.0	1.5	2.5	4.0
Senior Management	0.5	0.5	0.7	1.0	1.5
Support	0.2	0.2	0.3	0.5	0.7
Marketing (net of 6%)	1.5	3.0	4.0	5.0	6.0
Research	1.0	2.0	3.0	4.0	5.0
Client Service	1.5	6.0	12.0	22.0	41.0
Computer	0.5	0.8	1.5	2.2	6.0
Benefits	1.0	1.2	2.5	3.7	5.0
Head Office Rent	1.0	1.0	1.5	2.2	3.5
Total Operating Cost	8.0	16.7	27.0	43.1	72.7
Less Transfers	-3.5	-6.9	-12.0	-18.0	-32.7
Net Operating Cost	4.5	8.8	15.0	25.1	40.0
Operating Income	0.5	9.2	26.0	50.9	96.0
Operating Margin %	10%	51%	63%	67%	71%

NEXT STEPS

	STEP	WHO	WHEN
1	Develop coherent rationale for choosing ACL as a partner with which to build a mutual funds business in Potential Land		15/1
2	Create initial product design concepts and relative amount of funds raised by each product in first year		15/1
3	Develop rationale for the growth of the Potential Land economy, corporate profits, and equity market(s)		15/1
4	Develop organization & staffing concept, including approximate costs		15/1
5	Define cost structure (operating and capital)		15/1
6	Obtain rough perspective on systems and hardware		15/1
7	Develop rationale for being able to raise $500 million in first 6 months		15/1
8	Develop customer service system concept, including requirements for 'Monthly" purchase product		15/1
9	Develop outline marketing program and budget		15/1

The end products of these steps will provide the basis for developing:
1 The final strategic plan;
2 A detailed implementation plan: and
3 Appropriate narrative.

Chapter 5 - What You Learned

You learned a great deal in the course of reading this book. Let's review the most important items, including how to:

1 Focus on Winning

2 Get your management team to Understand, Believe, and Commit

3 Use approximations

4 Concentrate on logic, not detailed statistics

5 Focus on the right target

6 Create a strategic framework

7 Determine the Key Influences on Growth

8 Analyze the competition, including strengths and weaknesses

9 Determine the Basis of Competition

10 Evaluate customer behavior

11 Determine your own Strengths and Weaknesses, including why this comes relatively late in the process

12 Assess the impact of Market Maturity

13 Use Competitive Position Analysis to identify where you need to improve performance

14 Select the best strategy to use in your situation

15 Establish the key assumptions to track changes in the market and progress towards your goal

<u>1 Focus on Winning</u>

You may say "There he goes again, preaching about winning". Yes, you are right. However, it is the most important mindset in business. It allows you to prioritize all of the activities of your company. It allows you to work through each of the stages of strategy development.

For example, once you have determined the Basis of Competition, you can use it as a very handy guide to determine the relative importance of an action. If an action strengthens your hand against one or more of the factors on the Basis of Competition, that action will assist you in winning. If it is legal, it is likely to be a good thing. If it does not meet this test, then you have to question whether it is important, or even worth doing.

<u>2 Get your Management Team to Understand, Believe, and Commit</u>

Unless you can achieve this, your new strategy is likely to fail. Why, because without their whole-heated and enthusiastic support, the company will dither and never develop the drive to punch through to victory. And, you learned that the best way to achieve understanding, belief, and commitment with your management team is to have them directly involved in developing your new strategy. They will understand the compelling logic how it was put together. They will believe it is correct because they have seen it evolve from a blank piece of paper and tracked every step in its evolution. They will have been able to test their assumptions or objections in an open forum where fact, not opinion rules. And, as their colleagues and associates commit themselves to the new strategy, they will as well.

3 Use Approximations

Most people are reluctant to use approximations. Generations of teachers and professors have conditioned them to believe that there is only ONE right answer and that they should not guess at an answer because it most likely would be WRONG. Virtually every strategy development team over the years has been capable of making approximations that are amazingly useful. The reason for this is that when the various pieces and parts get fitted into the strategic framework, any glaring mistakes become obvious. There are built-in cross-checks and various methods of calibration so that the data becomes more and more accurate.

The other major point to make is that typically numbers have more to do with things like "The market has to be at least X to support a good business. The key question is: Is it currently X or better? How much better than X is gravy. This is the kind of analysis that makes sense. Grater precision is nice to have, but we don't have to have greater precision in order to move forward. It is important to remember that we can't measure the future. We can set up reasonable assumptions and then track events as the future unfolds.

4 Concentrate on Logic, not detailed statistics

Throughout this book, the following point has been emphasized: If you spend your time trying to make certain that the logic foots up, down and across, you seldom will go wrong. When the numbers to not make sense within your logic structure, double check the logic structure. When you are certain that that is reasonably correct, take a look at the critical numbers to find the disconnect. That will give you a strong indication on where the discrepancy is.

Markets behave according to their own internal logic. It is your job to figure out what that is. You have learned how to use four valuable tools, each of which are discussed later in this section: Basis of Competition, Market Maturity, Competitive Position, and Strategic Choice. These tools will help you construct and test the logic structure of the market you are examining. They are not absolutely foolproof – nothing is. But they are very valuable tools to apply in short-cutting the analytical process.

5 Focus on the Right Target

Before you can build your logic structure to explain why your market behaves the way it does, you must be certain that your are focused on ONE and only one complete market. You have learned how to do this and why it is important. If your focus is too narrow and you leave significant pieces of the market outside of your strategic analysis, you will be blind-sided, just our friends in the frozen baked sweet goods market were when people they were not tracking, or even considered to be competitors, took away over 80% of the market.

The other risk on not focusing on the right target is going too broadly. This will include businesses or parts of businesses with which you are not competing. If you divert your company's attention to attempt to compete with them, you will waste your time and resources. You will take resources away from programs and activities that will increase your chances of winning in your core market and you will reduce your chances of winning by spending scarce resources on peripheral issues. Stay focused on the main opportunity.

6 Create a Strategic Framework

Your strategic framework will evolve as you proceed through the strategy development process. Step-by-step, as you will build it, you will come closer to a coherent whole. Use this as you move forward to test the elements of the strategic framework as you work through the analysis. You will find that you are able to strengthen your understanding of the underlying logic that drives the market in which you are trying to win.

7 Determine the Key Influences on Growth

When you understand the key influences that are driving the growth of your market, up or down), you will have another set of insights into how to win. These come in a variety of form. For example, in the case study we went though earlier in this book, there were several very pertinent clues as to how you could take advantage of several of the key influences driving growth to achieve a competitive advantage. For example:

- Abolition of wealth tax, decrease on corporate and individual tax rates: The wealth tax, as well as lack of confidence in paper money was one of the powerful reasons why such a large proportion of personal savings was in gold and stored at home. It was much harder for the government to discover and tax these caches. It was unlikely that there would be an enormous conversion of gold to currency, but new additions to personal savings would begin to be invested in securities. But a huge element in this conversion was increasing the level of confidence of the investing public that securities investments would be "secure".

- High transaction costs - 1% brokerage / custody 0.7% / Stamp tax 0.5%: No one likes to be ripped off. A 2.2% transaction cost is high enough to discourage a large number of people. Particularly at a time when automated securities trading fees were as low as 5¢ per share. This certainly pointed toward the importance of automation and significant investment in technology.

- Very high spreads: This was particularly important in redemption charges. For an investor to lose between 20% and 40% of the value of his portfolio simply to redeem it, was unconscionable. Again, good technology and a general philosophy of fair treatment for customers was a powerful clue as how to capitalize on trends in the market to gain a strong competitive advantage.

8 Analyze the Competition, including strengths and weaknesses

Competitive Analysis is the key ingredient in developing the Basis of Competition. The simple part of the formula is that under normal circumstances, something should not be a part of the Basis of Competition unless one or more of the winners is doing it. Under normal circumstances. The case study you have just finished is one of those exceptions. Because of the fact that the market for mutual funds was restricted to government companies for so long, the leaders were in fact just the only participants. Their leadership was established by government fiat.

Many of the practices that customers find so objectionable grew up during the existence of the oligopoly. Otherwise these competitors would never have gotten away with what they did to exploit the investing public.

8 Analyze the Competition (Cont'd.)

Competitive Analysis is something that should be done on an ongoing basis. Markets change; competitors change. These need to be monitored on an ongoing basis. Also, salesmen can pick up an amazing amount of information just by listening carefully and asking the occasional question. This information needs to be added to the competitor profiles whenever something useful turns up.

9 Determine the Basis of Competition

It has been emphasized that you should set "Winning" as your business goal. And, you should aim to win in a market or large segment of the market where winning will generate substantial returns. Your motto should be "Play to Win and Win Where Winning is Worthwhile". The key to doing this is the Basis of Competition.

A tremendous amount hangs off the Basis of Competition. Using the current buzzwords, it is the capstone event of the Competitive Analysis. It is the summation of everything you have learned during that phase of the work. It also brings into play everyone's experience in working in your business: dealing with customers, watching the development of the market, talking with people, and your own observations.

If you only get one thing right, this is IT!

It is a wonderful tool to use from day-to-day decision making to determining the long-term direction of the company. The operative test is answering the simple question: "Does this strengthen the company against the Basis of Competition significantly, or does it not?" If it does, and is affordable, it may be a good thing. If it doesn't, and it costs anything in time, talent or money, then it clearly is a BAD thing. It's just as simple as that.

10 Evaluate Customer Behavior

Customer behavior is one of the most important clues about converting leads into sales and what is likely to affect the future of the market. For example, in our case study, we found out that only 15 - 25% of those who own shares have purchased mutual funds. Owning shares is the first and major step in getting people to invest in the securities market. That means that the other 75% to 85% of share owners are potential investors in mutual funds. That is, if you can make mutual fund ownership an attractive proposition. That is a big clue to what you need to do to develop the market.

Another thing you learned was that your potential customers fall into two age categories. Under 30, and over 50. The under 30s are saving to finance the children's education and marriages. The over 50s have taken care of these needs and are saving for themselves. Research shows that these are two different motivations. Your can translate these facts into sales.

11 Determine Your Company's Strengths and Weaknesses

This comes relatively late in the process and you learned that this important for several reasons. First, you want to be outward focused on the market place. Starting with your own company generally leads to an "Us vs. Them" concentration. Generally speaking, the analytical process leading up to the creation of the Basis of Competition becomes severely compromised if you start with a discussion of "what we are good at" or "what we like to do". There is an all to common tendency to describe the world as how one would like it to be, rather than how it really is out there. When it comes time to look inside, you have created a perspective on what key strengths and weaknesses are.

12 Assess the Impact of Market Maturity

You learned that Market Maturity represents the major factors that determine the dynamics at work in a specific market. The chart on the next page depicts the factors that operate during a specific dimension of market maturity. These change significantly as a market matures. Unlike biological maturity, market maturity can reverse itself, something that scientists of every dimension have been seeking since the origin of the Fountain of Youth myth.

The most important aspect of Market Maturity is the impact it has on corporate actions. Actions taken prematurely or too late can lead to disaster. We reviewed the case of Texas Instruments foray into electronic watches. In the early days of the market, LED technology ruled the roost. TI decided to get a jump on the market and built a large manufacturing facility dedicated to LED technology. Unfortunately, just as the factory, with production lines dedicated to LED technology was completed, the technology shifted to LCD, which used far less power and featured extended battery life. Competitors who had hung back and waited for the technology to "mature" were rewarded.

When you assess the maturity of your own market, you are generating valuable clues as to how your company should act. Combined with the other tools you have learned to use as you worked through the case study, you now have a powerful portfolio of tools at your disposal.

13 Use Competitive Position

Another really powerful tool you have learned to use through the case study analysis is Competitive Position ranking. This succinct analysis of where your company stands compared to its competitors distills out the areas where you can make the most progress in improving your performance.

You can use it as a tracking devices to measure the impact that competitors make to improve their position relative to your company. This gives you a tool that you can use to monitor where you stand in the race to achieve a winning position in the marketplace.

<u>14 Select the Best Strategy</u>

You also learned how to handle Strategic Choice. You learned that different strategies normally operate better, or are more likely to succeed, at different stages of Market Maturity. You can use this tool to update your strategy if circumstances change. You don't want to change horses too frequently and only if it is not working, for reasons other than it is not being implemented properly. If there is a radical change in the market, then you may want to revisit the question of what should be your primary strategy.

Remember, each of the strategies can be used two ways: first, as a primary strategy, and second, as a support strategy. In our case study, Technological Efficiency is used as a support strategy to develop the systems and infrastructure to provide superior client service. In this way it supported the primary strategy of Market Penetration – building the highest share possible before the market matured.

<u>15 Establish the Key Assumptions</u>

No one can consistently and accurately predict the future. Therefore, we need to be able to estimate what impact the evolution of the market, either from its slow and steady progression, or when a radical change in major factors affecting the market. Normally, you make these assumptions about the economy, or that portion of it which affects your market, your market itself, price and cost trends, key influences on growth, and Market Maturity. Other factors may come into play, depending on the market being served.

In our case study, we established key assumptions about the economy: national growth would be in the 5 to 6% range, and that 30% to 40% of excess corporate funds would be invested in mutual funds as these developed more specialized approaches. We also assumed that the government would continue to support "ethical" mutual funds, push deregulation, and privatization. We also assumed that the market would become more competitive as it becomes more sophisticated and competition increases.

We assumed that the market would be relatively easy to enter if one has capital and credibility, and that foreign companies will continue to play a major role, especially for new entrants needing to bolster their appeal to customers

The Mutual Fund Industry is assumed to grow at between 25% and 30% annually over the plan period (in fact it grew at 30% annually for over 10 years). Competitors will aggressively try to build their total assets under management. Prices were assumed to be stable for fees, while redemption rates would become swifter and far closer to actual NAV. Costs will generally decline because of improved technology and economies of scale. Social trends would shift away from gold to investment in securities becoming more popular.

Finally, it was assumed that Market Maturity will remain early to mid- growth.

Section 4, which follows, shows you how to apply what you have learned to the situations outlined in the introduction.

Chapter 6 - How to Apply You Learned to
the Situations in the Introduction

The purpose of this section is to describe how to apply this strategy development process to the situations described at the beginning of this book. Having gone through the case study, you now understand how the process works and you can see how it will apply in each case.

Transition to the next generation (1 and 2):

Situation: You are the head of a successful family owned business. You are approaching the age when you want to retire and do something else with your life. You also want to be around long enough that you can step in if problems develop. You need to provide clear direction for the next generation of family members who are going to take over or are going to serve on the internal board of the company. In an alternate scenario, you have carved off pieces of the business over the years, so that each member of the next generation has a piece to "run". This has made the company very unwieldy and there are questions as to whether all of the pieces make sense any more. The company needs to be streamlined. But, you need to bring the family members and the key managers along so you know that they understand how the new plan was put together, believe that it is the correct way to go, and will commit themselves to the implementation of "their" new plan.

How to undertake either of these tasks? Experience shows that the strategy development team should be expanded to include the family members and the key non-family managers who will play a key role in the future of the company. This is true even if some of the people on the team will play a passive role. In most of the situations of this type, the number of next generation of family members is small in a first / second generation transition with one patriarch involved. In a second / third generation transition, 2 to 4 times as many family members can be involved.

The absolute number of family members related to the company is not important. What is important is that every family member who is going to be involved in the company, whether as a manager, as a board member, or a beneficiary, must be involved in developing the strategy. You do not want to create and "In" group and an "Out" group. Involvement generally leads to a much more harmonious relationship between family members, between family members and management, and will facilitate the orderly development of the company. This situation places a special burden on person conducting the strategy development work. It is all too easy for participants to suspect the leader of pushing his or her point of view. Therefore, you need to choose the project leader very carefully.

In case number #2, sorting out what to keep and what to eliminate, you will be well advised to be very thorough in your SBU analysis as that will probably set up a situation that will create controversy. Then, you should track through one business at a time. If time does not permit tracking through each business completely, carry the analysis at least through the Basis of Competition. A little extra time in doing the job thoroughly can save years of wrangling and acrimony. What you need to remember is that sorting the pieces and parts out, and concentrating on the most powerful ones creates a more successful company, which is in the long-term best interest of all of the family members.

Promotion Provokes Need for Focus (3)

You just got promoted to run a part of your company. Some pieces seem to fit, and others don't. You need to figure how to organize the pieces and parts so they fit into a pattern that makes sense in terms of how the market or possibly – the various markets work. How do you sort this out?

The methodology for reaching a solution is much clearer than the politics. The analytical approach is similar to that described in Case #2 – sort out the businesses. However, in this case the SBU analysis is as far as you need to go for everything other than the core business. Hopefully there is one. Carry through to the conclusion for the core business and pursue the others just far enough to be able to demonstrate that they are different and that the other pieces reside in other divisions.

Hopefully, the companion parts in just one other division. Then, it might be possible to agree on a swap: you get some of the pieces to make up a whole, and the other division gets some of your pieces so that everyone ends up with complete businesses. This makes a great deal of sense for the parent, as well as for the siblings. Hopefully logic can solve this problem, leaving the overall company stronger.

Handling a Turnaround (4)

You just got handed a business that is in a real mess. It's like the old De Soto division at Chrysler – any young manager who showed great promise was sent over to run it. Each burned out, and left the company. You don't want this to happen to you. But, you also need to bring the management team you just inherited along with you on your new journey. How do you figure out how to fix the business and get the management team to join in with you?

It is very likely that the management team is fractured, and has divided in various camps espousing different solutions. To a great extent, this causes the management paralysis gripping the business. You have to draw them together behind one solution. The strategy development process is the ideal tool to get this done because management disagreements about which route to take get dealt with during the analysis phase of the work. Don't try to resolve the conflicts in isolation. What really counts is how all of the pieces of the strategic puzzle fit together. Sometimes an ideal solution for a small part of the business looks very good until you see what it does to everything else. Remember what our friend Clausewitz said about concentration of effort: The strategy must focus on the most important goal, the one that will have the greatest impact on success.

Generally speaking, in a turnaround, the peripheral stuff needs to be shoved to the side, discarded or put on ice until the main problem is solved. Focus only on the core business and get that to be successful. In this case the best solution for all the other pieces is clearly the enemy of implementing a good plan for the core business with promptness and vigor.

As momentum builds towards successfully implementing the plan to solve the main problem, you will find that the management team becomes more united. They will see why the choices that we made were correct and that they are working successfully.

We Know Our Business so Well, We Don't Need to Plan (5)

You work in a company that plans informally and the seat of the pants style seems to be wearing a bit thin. You want to volunteer to create a formal strategy to lift the business to a higher level. But, you need to convince your boss to let you take a swing at creating a winning strategy. This book will help you convince the boss that you know how to do it!

This is very common when a business is small or it was small when its founder developed it. He remembers when he knew where every tool was on the rack (long since gone), and he knew every customer. If you want to be successful in convincing him to go through the strategy development process, simplify the outline in the appendix. You can always add things back in if they become relevant as you go through the first working session. Alternatively, during the interim period between the first and second working sessions, you can review the draft strategic framework document and see what to be put back in. This is not an ideal solution, but if you are dealing with a founder who is basing his decisions what the world was like when he started off, you need to remember two things:

- He deserves a great deal of respect for what he has accomplished; and

- The world really has changed since then.

There is no sense in fighting up front about what has changed. You will lose. But, if you can convince him to go through the process, it can be a virtually pain free, evolutionary way to learn about the new reality.

This is Strange Territory – I Need A Map! (6)

You have just been through a case study illustrating how to handle this situation. It is a little more cumbersome than developing a strategic plan with a seasoned and knowledgeable team for a single business that they know well. You may want to bring in a few outside experts (never just 1!), or a specialized consulting firm. Use them as resources, not to drive the analysis. Otherwise, your team will be marginalized.

Maybe I Do Need to Measure the World (7)

You run a large company with several divisions and business units operating in many countries, and you suspect that each may have different market conditions. You want to make certain that each significant market is being addressed properly, but you don't want to spend millions doing it. And you want country management to be deeply involved and committed to the results of the project.

There are two levels to this project. First of all, you need to train a team execute a "quick and dirty" survey of the most important group of businesses serving a market that has a number of element in common. It is important that the team, typically two people, survey all of the units involved in the review of each business. That way the differences will become far more identifiable and more accurately diagnosed than if you send out written instructions to each unit and try to piece together results from their written reports. Boots on the ground and all that.

There have been a number of these projects, and the results have been fascinating. One was for an international pharmaceutical company operating around the globe. They had a division focused on animal health. Their strategy process had been set up by one of the world's most prestigious consulting firms. This firm had broken the market out into two segments: Ectocides (you apply it to the outside of the animal, and Endocides (you get the stuff inside the animal – typically in its food or by injections). Even if you broke down the markets more finely, such as differentiating between the market for Sheep Dip and Cattle Tickicides (kills ticks), there were still significant differences. Even then, you would have thought that the single product businesses were uniform in every market in which they operated. Absolutely wrong! The results were widely different from market to market. By the time the examination of each country completed the Basis of Competition analysis, the differences became clear. Take one of their products – Tickicides. Take two neighboring countries - Brazil and Argentina. The cattle were about the same. The client was very successful in one country, and a dismal failure in the other, where the management was constantly being beaten up and replaced.

What was the problem? And, it became readily apparent when the same pairs of eyes looked at both markets. In one country, cattle were marketable if the ticks had not consumed the entire animal. In the other country, if only a few ticks were found, the cattle could not be sold. Not surprisingly, superb efficacy at a somewhat affordable price was the most important product characteristic in one country, and low price was vital in the other. The product that fit one country's market failed miserably in the other.

What's the moral? Do a quick survey. Make the comparisons. Draw the conclusions and decide whether a "one size fits all" worldwide strategy, or a country by country approach makes the most sense. If the country by country approach makes the most sense, do a thorough strategy development project for each major business in each country. Upon reaching this conclusion, one client exclaimed "Our businesses are very simple. What's complicated is that we have so many of them!"

Apples and Oranges (8)

You have just gotten involved with a large merger and you need to sort out and the pieces and parts. You need to decide whether the existing structures need to remain separate, or are if there are pieces that need to be combined with one or more of those from the acquisition into larger and more powerful wholes. The first question is do any of these pieces naturally fit together, or will the force fit approach end up combining apples and oranges in the interest of organizational symmetry.

The hierarchy of answers is something like this:

1 If two pieces are part of the same SBU in the same country, then they should be combined and a joint strategy developed. This also will tend to integrate the two management teams.

2 If two pieces have many things in common as a result of your SBU analysis, except that the serve different country markets, they should get their own strategies, but they may be administered in their host countries as makes logical and economic sense.

3 If some of the pieces in different countries are different SBUs from anything else in the country, then run them through the strategy development process to determine what is the best-case scenario for each of these businesses. If this results in an attractive business, keep it and develop it. If not, sell it off and retain just those parts that make sense to keep.

If It's Too Dense to Read, Maybe They'll Think Its Thorough (9)

You have just received a monstrous volume that is represented to be a strategic plan. There is an enormous amount of data included. However, you are not certain that it really gets to the point of what is needed to underpin a successful strategy. Often verbose, longwinded plans get lost in their own verbiage and lose any sense of logical internal organization.

Print out a few copies of the strategy development outline. If you have the leverage, sit down with the authors and ask them to place the various pieces and parts in the outline. If not, then lay down the plan and the outline next to each other and try to track through to find the sections listed in the outline.

Based on this analysis, you can put together a reasoned, substantive critique that can serve as the guide to focusing the draft plan on those things that really important. The watchwords are Clarity and Focus.

Appendices

1 Overall outline of the strategy development process

2 SBU determination memo

3 Market Maturity Definition chart

4 Competitive Position blank exercise chart. This chart allows your strategy development team to work through the elements of the Competitive Position ranking system to try to figure out for themselves into which phase of Market Maturity each is applicable.

5 Competitive Position answer sheet

6 Competitive Position Criteria Definitions

7 Natural Period of Strategy Execution work sheet. This chart allows your strategy development team to work through the elements of the Natural Period of Strategy Execution to try to figure out for itself into which phase of Market Maturity each strategy most likely to operate effectively. This speeds up the learning.

8 Natural Period of Strategy Execution answer sheet

9 Strategy definitions and descriptions

10 Getting Started List of Steps

Appendix 1

OUTLINE OF THE STRATEGY DEVELOPMENT PROCESS

The purpose of this guide is to provide a summary outline of some of the main elements considered in developing the strategic management capability and strategic plan for an individual Strategic Business Unit (SBU).

I. INDUSTRY DEFINITION:

A Definition of Scope: Clearly state how much of the corporation is being profiled for strategic management. For example, the ABC Division, domestic operations only.

B. Vital Statistics for the SBU:

1. Absolute sales (revenue) volume, current year and as a percent of corporate total.

2. Absolute net assets, current year and as a percent of corporate total.

3. Absolute profits, current year and as a percent of corporate total.

4. Capital Employed:

a. Uses: Fixed assets, working capital, etc.

b. Corporate Sources: debt, equity, non- and off-balance sheet and approximate costs and effective corporate tax rate

C. Market segment(s) in which the SBU is currently competing, for example, the specialty X market. (Be careful to define the market segment so that it properly describes the nature of the current business.) Also, state, if desired, the future market segment(s) in which the SBU plans or hopes to compete.

D. Products/services provided and end-use if needed for clarification. For example, product/service X for commercial use.

E. If the numbers above include the sale of less important products not described by the words, so state and footnote any significant skewing of the numbers. For example, minor products/services not discussed include product M and service N with no significant skewing of the overall data.

F. SBU Analysis (See separate instructions)

II. BUSINESS EVALUATION:

A. Industry Description: the industry is defined as those firms competing directly or indirectly with the SBU.

1. Dollar size of the total industry.

2. Growth over time (by segments, if necessary, and in relationship to the GNP), both in historical and future units and dollars.

3. Key influences on the growth (or shrinkage) of the market.

4. Cyclicality (tied to specific industry indicators).

5. Seasonality (% of the business by quarter or period).

6. Competition (if not handled above):

    a.   Number of competitors - increasing or decreasing?

    b.   Names and market shares of current major competitors (quantified to the extent possible).

    c.   How is the leader's share changing - relative to the SBU?

    d.   Industry stability - entrants versus failures.

    e.   Foreign competition (size and growth).

7. How important is this industry or industry segment to the SBU's competitors (e.g., relative profitability, emotional commitment)?

8. Organizational nature of competition (free standing company or division).

9. Degree of integration, forward or backward (e.g., leaders are integrated from raw material to final product).

10. Competitor strengths and weaknesses, and strategic thrust as perceived in the marketplace.

11. Product line concept and unique values offered (specialty/commodity matrix).

12. Basis of Competition (e.g., price/service/technology, key factors for success).

13. Barriers to entry.

14. Production and distribution facilities status:

a.   Industry capacity situation, current year by percent utilization.

    b.   What is optimum capacity utilization.

    c.   Minimum economic size of incremental increase to existing plant capacity and for entirely new plant.

    d.   Start-up time required to build and bring on stream incremental new plant and to start up new plant.

    e.   Who is planning new capacity and when will it come on stream.

15. Product vulnerability:

a.   To new product/service.

    b.   To elimination of need.

16. Normal distribution channels.

17. Role of technology over time (product/process).

18. Constraints (community / regulatory).

19. Financial operating characteristics and trends, e.g.,

a. Capital employed: equity, debt, non- and off-balance sheet, other capital

b. Profit economics: profitability, fixed versus variable costs, break-even analysis, leverage factors

c. Capital factors: debt capacity, capital intensity, critical mass of investment required

d. Corporate Sources: debt, equity, non- and off-balance sheet and approximate costs and effective corporate tax rate

20. Price trends (e.g., are industry prices dispersed among competitors; is there a price leader; if so, who?).

21. Sales terms and level of accounts receivable (if available and pertinent).

22. Profit improvement opportunities immediately apparent.

B. Market Description: The market is defined as those customers served by the industry, either directly, indirectly, or both:

1. Size of market segments and growth trends.

2. Key changes and trends in the market.

3. Geographic distribution of the market.

4. Price trends.

5. Customers served by market, segmented by type:

a. Categories, e.g., consumers, retailers, wholesalers, OEM, further converters of product, etc.

b. Specific identification by kind and actual industries (name).

c. Demand sensitivity for foreign goods.

d. Degree of concentration (e.g., by geography, by size, by other particular characteristics).

C. Business Unit Description: (as defined in the Strategic Business Unit Definition Guide).

1. Share of industry over time.

2. Share(s) of market(s) and appropriate segments.

3. Breadth of product line versus competition.

4. Degree of customer concentration.

5. Strengths and weaknesses (e.g., a particular function or process) that may or not be a competitive strength or weakness.

6. How did the corporation enter the industry or industry segment and why.

7. Technological strength versus competition.

8. The extent to which the market values corporate and/or brand name.

9. Channels of distribution.

10. Possession of sufficient volume to justify the optimal distribution system for the industry.

11. Present level of and potential for international business by percent of sales.

12. Degree of integration, forward and backward.

13. Production facilities status:

a.   Capacity situation, current year by percent utilization.

b.   What is optimum for SBU?

c.   Other profitable uses?

14. Financial operating characteristics and trends, e.g.,

a.   Capital employed: equity, debt, non- and off-balance sheet, other capital

b.   Profit economics: profitability, fixed versus variable costs, break-even analysis, leverage factors

c.   Capital factors: debt capacity, capital intensity, critical mass of investment required

d.   Capital map: capital employed in business (raw materials and other input inventories, receivables, production facilities, distribution, business premises, other

e.   Economic Value added: Estimated capital employed at estimated cost of capital versus operating profit after tax

15. Total cost position compared with competitors.

16. Profit improvement opportunities

17. Potential blue sky opportunities (any major opportunities not included in the current plan).

D. Maturity of the Industry's Markets:
1. Examples of maturity.
2. Determination of maturity relevant to the SBU.
E. Competitive Position:
1. Competitive position ranking exercise.
2. Compared to competition:
a.   Dominant.

b.   Strong.

c.   Favorable.

d.   Satisfactory.

e.   Weak.

f.   Non-viable.

III. STRATEGY SELECTION
A. Strategy Selection:
1. Strategy Definition Guide.
2. Past and current strategy classification.
3. Strategy periodicity exercise.
B. Key Assumptions:
1. Economy:
a.   National growth.

b.   Degree of government influence.

c.   Competitive climate.

2. Industry.
a.   Growth.

b.   Stability.

c.   Competitor actions.

d.   Growth of the markets from which demand is derived.

    e. Potential threats (e.g., technological obsolescence).

    f. Capital employed and economic value added

3. Market:
a. Price trends.

b. Cost trends (including labor).

4. Influences on the Market
a. Corporate or group pressures (e.g., impact of previous and present corporate strategy, capital policy, hurdle rates, etc.).

b. Labor climate.

c. Social trends (e.g, consumerism, equal opportunity, etc.).

d. Government.

C. Market Maturity (Similar to past and current industry maturity section).
D. Future business strategies (similar to past and current strategies section).
E. Specific programs with key target dates:
1. List of the major programs that are necessary to execute strategy.
2. Where possible, show cost/benefit summary.
3. Profit improvement program
4. Capital utilization program
F. Major issues to be resolved by SBU and Group/Corporate (summarize critical decisions so that priorities are clear).
G. Interdivisional factors related to plan
1. Kind of dependency on other organizational units.
2. Degree of dependency on other organizational units.
3. Benefits provided by SBU to other organizations.
H. Acquisition criteria.
1. Past criteria for acquisitions made.
2. Desired criteria for future acquisitions needed to implement strategy.
IV. STRATEGY ASSESSMENT
A. Past financial performance versus past strategy.
1. How close has the past financial performance followed past strategy, describe and make judgment as to whether:

a. Consistent;

b. Not consistent.

2. Significant changes in past performance numbers (including reasons - what went wrong).
3. Profit improvement opportunities.
4. Economic value added.
B. Data assessment.
C. Style of management analysis: Assess primary characteristics in terms of:
1. Planning:
a. Time frame.

b. Format.

c. Degree of corporate uniformity.

d. Procedure at each level.

2. Organizing/Structure & Compensation.
a. Degree of choice in structure.

b. Degree of flexibility in compensation.

3. Communication system:
a. Description of method and style.

b. Degree of flexibility.

4. Controls and reporting:
a. System Description.

b. Performance criteria (fixed or adjustable).

c. Degree of detail.

5. Nature of climate:
a. Degree of formality.

b. Ties with the past.

  c. Sensitivity to changes.

  d. Ability to respond effectively to changes.

  e. Attitude towards risk taking.

 6. Actions required for congruency (steps to be taken so that the managerial system matches the strategic demands of the market).
  D. Risk analysis.

Appendix 2

STRATEGIC BUSINESS UNIT DEFINITION GUIDE

A Strategic Business Unit (SBU) is what might be referred to as a natural business. A natural business is a business 'segment' with an independent marketplace for goods or services. If the marketplace is independent, then one must develop a free-standing strategy for the SBU reflecting the realities of demand and competition in this marketplace. 'Averaging' or 'merging' this marketplace and the strategies for it into other SBUs will normally result in failure to achieve the objectives set for the SBU.

Therefore, correct definition of the SBU is essential to effective strategy development. The first step in strategy development is to determine whether the business segment under consideration is:

- An independent and inseparable natural business (i.e., a Strategic Business Unit); or

- More than one natural business or SBU; or

- A part of some larger SBU within the corporation,; or

- A functional activity (e.g., a manufacturing or research facility) that is a part of several SBUs and can not develop strategy without coordinating with the managers of each of the related SBUs.

The answer to this question can be established initially through the development of a set of clues (all of which must be considered) rather than any single criterion. The nature of the clues is founded on conditions in the marketplace, rather than production/cost linkages (e.g., common manufacturing facilities or methods of manufacturing), technical linkages (e.g., common technology), or common distribution channels.

Judgment is then applied to the determination of SBU status. When there is doubt as to the independence of a SBU, the safe choice is to treat it as part of a larger whole. This will prevent being blind-sided strategically. If, in the final analysis, it is not part of a larger marketplace, this will become readily apparent during subsequent strategy development. The ultimate test of SBU status is whether the market(s) being considered have a single Market Maturity, Competitive Position and Basis of Competition for which a single strategy can be developed.

The clues, which initially define an SBU, are:

1. Prices: Do price changes on any product within the business unit necessitate price changes on:

- All other products/services;

- Only on some other products/services;

- On products in other business units?

If all other products/services are affected, then the unit is probably one SBU. If only some products/services are affected, then this provides a clue that there are probably two or more SBUs within the unit. If the product pricing in another unit is affected, then the unit under consideration is probably part of another, or larger SBU.

2. Customers: Likewise, if the unit has a single set of customers, it is a single SBU. If it has multiple sets of customers, it may comprise more than one SBU. If it shares customers with another unit, it may be part of a SBU in that unit or a larger SBU.

3. Competitors: If the unit has a single set of competitors, it will tend to be a single SBU. If it competes against distinctly different sets of companies for different parts of its customer/industry spectrum, it may be more than one SBU.

4. Quality/Style: If a quality or styling change for any product necessitates a corresponding change in other products/services, then all these products/services will tend to be part of the same natural business. If product/service quality or styling changes have no impact on other products/services within the unit, then the unit is probably made up of more than one SBU.

5. Substitutability: If the products/services sold by the unit are substitutable, one for the other, this tends to indicate a single SBU. Other such substitutable products/services marketed by other units within the corporation would also tend to be in the same SBU.

6. Divestment or Liquidation: The most nebulous, but sometimes the most revealing, clue to test for SBU status is the impact that selling or dropping the product/service has on the marketing or selling effectiveness of the remaining products/services. If divestment or liquidation has some impact, then there are at least two SBUs within the unit. If the product pricing in another unit is affected, then the unit under consideration is probably part of another, or larger, SBU.

Appendix 3

Descriptor	Market Maturity Guide			
	Embryonic	Growth	Mature	Aging
Growth Rate	Percent growth in 100's; accelerating; meaningful rate can not be calculated	Percent growth in 10's; but constant or decelerating	Single digit growth; cyclical	Industry volume cycles by declines over long term
Industry Potential	Usually difficult to determine	Substantially exceeds Industry volume, but is subject to unforeseen developments	Well-known; primary markets approach saturation volume	Saturation is reached; no potential remains
Product Line Breadth	Basic Product line is established	Rapid proliferation as product lines are extended	Product turnover, but little or no change in breadth	Shrinking
Participants	Increasingly rapidly	Increasing to peak; followed by shakeout and consolidation	Stable	Declines; but business may break up into small co's.
Share Distribution	Volatile	A few firms have major shares; minor shares are unlikely to gain major shares	Firms with major shares are entrenched.	Concentration increases; or shares are dispersed to locals
Customer Loyalty	Little or none.	Some; buyers are aggressive.	Suppliers are well-known; buying patterns established.	Strong; number of alternatives decreases.
Ease of Entry	Usually easy, but opportunity may not be apparent.	Usually easy; the presence of competitors offset by vigorous growth.	Difficult; competitors are entrenched, and growth is slowing.	Difficult; little incentive.
Technology	Concept development and product engineering.	Product line refinement and extension.	Process and materials refinement; new product line development to renew growth.	Role is minimal.

Appendix 4

Competitive Position Rating System	Embryonic	Growth	Mature	Aging
1. To be strong on the Basis of Competition				
2. To have high share in your market				
3. To have an increasing market share				
4. To be gaining more points of share than the leader				
5. To be one of three companies with leading shares				
6. To have a protected market position, e.g. patents, etc.				
7. To have price leadership in your market				
8. To have a broad product line for your market				
9. To have a strong corporate and/or brand name				
10. To be free from dependence on few customers				
11. To have total costs that are low relative to competition				
12. To have lower variable manufacturing costs per unit				
13. To have sufficient volume to support optimal distribution				
14. To be operating at close to optimum capacity				
15. To have special relationships with other entities				
16. To have profitable alternatives for your production facilities				
17. To have production facilities larger than viable new units				
18. To have profitable operations				
19. To be producing a net cash flow				
20. To have as much forward integration as competitors				
21. To have as much backward integration as competitors				
22. To have a strong technology relative to competition				
23. To be capable of taking risks because of overall strength				
24. To have a managerial system supportive of risk taking				
25. To be able to quickly respond to external changes				
26. To have a business that is unattractive to competitors				

Appendix 5

Competitive Position Rating System	Embryonic ***	Growth (Some-times Applies)	Mature	Aging (Generally Applies)
1. To be strong on the Basis of Competition	▓	▓	▓	▓
2. To have high share in your market	▓	▓		
3. To have an increasing market share				
4. To be gaining more points of share than the leader				
5. To be one of three companies with leading shares	▓	▓		
6. To have a protected market position, e.g. patents, etc.	****			
7. To have price leadership in your market			▓	
8. To have a broad product line for your market		▓		
9. To have a strong corporate and/or brand name		****	▓	▓
10. To be free from dependence on few customers		****	▓	▓
11. To have total costs that are low relative to competition		****	▓	▓
12. To have lower variable manufacturing costs per unit				
13. To have sufficient volume to support optimal distribution		▓	▓	
14. To be operating at close to optimum capacity				
15. To have special relationships with other entities				
16. To have profitable alternatives for your production facilities				
17. To have production facilities larger than viable units		▓		
18. To have profitable operations		▓	▓	▓
19. To be producing a net cash flow			▓	▓
20. To have as much forward integration as competitors			▓	▓
21. To have as much backward integration as competitors			▓	▓
22. To have a strong technology relative to competition	▓	▓	▓	▓
23. To be capable of taking risks because of total strength	▓	▓		
24. To have a managerial system supportive of risk taking	▓	▓		
25. To be able to quickly respond to external changes	▓	****		
26. To have a business that is unattractive to competitors				

Appendix 6

Competitive Position Rating System Definitions

Ranking Factor #1 – To Be Strong on the Basis of Competition

Being strong on the Basis of Competition is the most important factor in the Competitive Position Ranking System. If you are very strong on this factor, you have a significant chance of winning. If you are not, get there or get out of the business if the market is Mid Growth to Aging phases. This factor cuts across all levels of Market Maturity.

Ranking Factor #2 - To have high share in your market

Other than by using a high degree of linguistic legerdemain, there is no way you can be a Winner if you do not have a high share of the market in which you are competing. Cuts across all levels of Market Maturity.

Ranking Factor #3 - To have an increasing market share

This is a common mistake in thinking about Competitive Position. The winner could have a 60% share and holding steady at that level. You could have doubled you share by going from 1% to 2%. You're still not the winner. If you are taking 10 share points a year from the leaders, it is reasonable that you should get a plus.

Ranking Factor #4 - To be gaining more points of share than the leader

Basically, the same logic as that for #3 holds – you could have gone from 1% to 2%, thereby doubling your share, while the winner could be static at 60%. There is no way you can be the winner at a 2% share.

Ranking Factor #5 - To be one of three companies with leading shares

Absolutely necessary to be one of three leading companies in terms of market share. As in 1 and 2 above, cuts across all levels of Market Maturity

Ranking Factor #6 - To have a protected market position, e.g. patents, etc

If this factor plays at all, it plays in embryonic, before the market fully develops. Generally speaking, by the time the market enters the growth phase, there are multiple ways to achieve whichever product attributes that are important and, with the exception of patented pharmaceuticals and a few other research-intensive products, the markets are generally fairly open.

Ranking Factor #7 - To have price leadership in your market

Price leadership, if it plays at all, is applicable during the Mature phase of a market, when production methods have standardized to the point that price, not performance becomes a major differentiator. The price leader typically has the power to force other competitors

Ranking Factor #8 - To have a broad product line for your market

This factor becomes important during the Growth Phase of a market, when it has not standardized on the few product variations for which demand is the greatest and the market is still in search mode. When it matures, several things happen: the leader has a relatively narrow product line limited to the high volume products, and the trailing companies are stuck with the low volume, and therefore, expensive products.

Ranking Factor #9 - To have a strong corporate and/or brand name

This factor can play in Growth, and does play in Mature and Aging, by which new strong names could have become established. When one looks at many of the new categories of consumer electronic products, the leading players are new companies. For example, IBM dropped out of the personal computer market.

Ranking Factor #10 - To be free from dependence on few customers

This factor is strongly influenced by the art of the possible. In embryonic, one may only have one customer. As the market moves into its growth phase, the number of customers will expand. If one does not have a broad customer base in Mature, your company is in trouble. By the time the market enters Aging, you are stuck with whoever is still a customer in a shrinking market.

Ranking Factor #11 - To have total costs that are low relative to competition

This is a very important concept. It is TOTAL COSTS that matter. Many times working with large multi-nationals that because of the application of their superior manufacturing technology have low costs at the local level, but by the time that several levels of overhead get layered on, their cost structure is no longer competitive. However, this is a factor that becomes important when the market becomes price competitive, typically during Mature

Ranking Factor #12 - To have lower variable manufacturing costs per unit

This is the corollary of number 11 above. Having lower variable manufacturing costs per unit is helpful, but it is total cost that counts.

Ranking Factor #13 - To have sufficient volume to support optimal distribution

Plays in the Growth and Mature phases when price competition begins to become the norm and therefore, effective management of costs becomes important. Also, you need to be able to cover the bulk of the market efficiently.

Ranking Factor #14 - To be operating at close to optimum capacity

This says very little about your company's position in the market. It speaks to your production capacity, which could have no relation to what the market needs or could buy.

Ranking Factor #15 - To have special relationships with other entities*

This factor, while often prized by company management, is normally illusory. Unless it is something that grants almost monopoly power, which could create problem with regulators, it means you are dependent on an external entity, which could come to dominate you. Not a source of strength for you.

Ranking Factor #16 - To have profitable alternatives for your production facilities

Why would you think that this is a source of strength? If you have profitable alternatives for your production facilities, why aren't you serving that market?

Ranking Factor #17 – To have production facilities larger than viable new units

This is only a source of strength during the early to mid phases of Growth because you can grow significantly without adding capacity, leverage fixed costs, and only have to concerned about variable costs. Presumably as you use more of the existing capacity, your margins should improve significantly.

Ranking Factor #18 – To have profitable operations

This plays significantly during the Growth, Mature and Aging phases of Market Maturity. During the ramp up phase in Embryonic, it is unlikely that your operation will be profitable form an accounting standpoint.

Ranking Factor #19 – To be producing a net cash flow

This is vital during Mature and Aging. It is generally not possible as you are investing in product development in Embryonic, nor during Growth, when the market is expanding and you are investing everything you can get your hands to support that growth.

Ranking Factor #20 – To have as much forward integration as competitors

This is a function of stability in the marketplace and finding the right scale. Buying up retail distribution is an example. Done prematurely, it is very easy to get the scale wrong and you end up with too much or too little of a good thing. If you have too little, you end up competing with your non-owned retailers, who will soon drop you. This operates during Mature and Aging.

Ranking Factor #21 – To have as much backward integration as competitors

Backward integration means moving down the distribution change towards your sources of raw materials or component manufacturing. During Mature, it can often allow you to achieve lower costs, but in Aging, it can mean that you have more capital tied up in capacity that you can't use.

Ranking Factor #22 – To have a strong technology relative to competition

Absolutely necessary during all phases of Market Maturity. The technology shifts from product technology, applicable during Embryonic and though to mid-Growth, to production technology from late Growth through to Aging, when the role of technology shifts to "make it faster, better, cheaper". However, it could be argued that there is effectively no role of technology in an Ageing market because you can buy up anything you need from those who have gone out of the business, and because the market is shrinking, it is unlikely anyone with invest in new technology.

Ranking Factor #23 – To be capable of taking risks because of overall strength

Capability to take risk does not mean that there is a willingness to take intelligent risks. Until the recent madness hit, large insurance companies were classic example of institutions that certainly had the capacity to take risk, but rarely if ever did so. This factor plays an important role in Embryonic and Growth, because these are the phases of Market Maturity during which risks frequently need to be taken. In contrast, companies competing in Mature markets typically have a well developed bureaucracy. They can afford to be ponderous because the market does not change very rapidly, so they can study, assess and procrastinate without danger.

Ranking Factor #24 – To have a managerial system supportive of risk taking

Applies during Embryonic and Growth. Useless unless it is combined with the capability to take risk. However, absent this factor, as described above, the willing to take risks is not very useful unless the company has the resources necessary to do so.

Ranking Factor #25 – To be able to quickly respond to external changes

Applies during Embryonic and Growth. These are phases of Market Maturity during which one can go home on Friday and when one comes back in on Monday, the world has changed. By late Growth, the market has calmed down a bit and possessing this capability is less vital to success.

Ranking Factor #26 – If it is unattractive to your competitors, why is it attractive to you? One could argue that this is a variant of the "protected position" concept, essentially it says that you are protected because you are in a really lousy business. Find something better to do with your time and your capital.

Appendix 7

The purpose of the exercise is to illustrate that different strategies work best at different levels of Market Maturity. Form your team into small groups of 2 to 3. Give each person a copy of the following blank sheet on which to record their individual answers after everyone is done, pass out the answer sheet and discuss the results.

Natural Period of Strategy Execution

	Embryonic	Growth	Mature	Aging
A. Initial Market Development				
B. Market Penetration				
C. Same Product/Same Market				
D. Same Product/New Market				
E. New Product/Same Market				
F. New Product/New Market				
G. Backward Integration				
H. Forward Integration				
I. Export Same Product				
J. Licensing Abroad				
K. Development of Overseas Facilities				
L. Development of Overseas Business				
M. Excess Capacity				
N. Market Rationalization				
O. Distribution Rationalization				
P. Product Line Rationalization				
Q. Production Rationalization				
R. Technological Efficiency				
S. Methods & Functions				
T. Traditional Cost Cutting				
U. Hesitation				
V. Little Jewel				
W. Pure Survival				
X. Unit Abandonment				

Appendix 8

Natural Period of Strategy Execution

	Embry-onic	Growth	Mature	Aging
A. Initial Market Development	xxxxxxx	xxxxx		
B. Market Penetration	xxxxxx	xxxxx		
C. Same Product/Same Market		xxxx	xxxxxx	xxxx
D. Same Product/New Market	xxxx	xxxxxxx	xxxx	
E. New Product/Same Market		xxxx	xxxx	
F. New Product/New Market			xxxxxx	
G. Backward Integration		xx	xxxxxx	
H. Forward Integration			xxxxxx	
I. Export Same Product		xxxxx	xxxx	
J. Licensing Abroad	xxxx	xxxxx		
K. Development of Overseas Facilities		xxxxx	xxxxxx	
L. Development of Overseas Business		xxxx	xxxx	
M. Excess Capacity		xxxxx		
N. Market Rationalization		xxxx	xxxxxx	
O. Distribution Rationalization		xxxx	xxxxxx	
P. Product Line Rationalization		xxxxx	xxxxxx	
Q. Production Rationalization			xxxxxx	xxxxxx
R. Technological Efficiency		xxxxx	xxxxxx	
S. Methods & Functions			xxxxxx	xxxxxx
T. Traditional Cost Cutting			xxxxxx	xxxxxx
U. Hesitation			xxxxxx	xxxxxx
V. Little Jewel			xxxxxx	xxxxxx
W. Pure Survival				xxxxxx
X. Unit Abandonment	xxxxxx			xxxxxx

Appendix 9

Definition of the Alternative Strategies
A Initial Market Development
To invest in creating a primary demand for a product new to a large number of customers
Probable consequences:
- Very high initial marketing & sales expenses with minimal short-term profits (or significant losses)

- Increased receivables as trade credit may be used and a marketing tool

- Impacts on P&L more than on Balance Sheet

- Negative cash flow

Requires:
- Continued high technical service and application engineering

- Large expense budget

Risk:
- Highest since parameters of the market are unknown

B Market Penetration
To increase market share through manipulation of the marketing mix,; e.g., lower price, product line breadth, increased product and sales service, increased advertising
Probable Consequences:
- Lowered profit margins

- Short term sales growth directed at increasing market share

- Increased receivables

- Increased fixed assets due to increased capacity requirements

- Lowered unit costs in the long term

Requires
- Increased marketing and selling expenses

- Increased working capital

- Increased capital investment if increased capacity is required

- Willingness to sacrifice short-term earnings in the hope of longer-term success

Risk: High
C Maintenance (also called Same Product / Same Market)
To execute the those strategies required to maintain the present competitive position of the existing business unit … with the existing products in existing markets
Probable Consequences:
- Increased sales volume … at the rate of industry growth

- Profit margins will remain stable near-term and probably decline over time

- Decreased working capital over time

- Increased cash throw off

- Lowered unit costs if plan and distribution system are not already loaded

Requires:
- Investment in strategies to hold competitive position

Risk:
- Low

D Same Product / New Market
To expand the existing domestic market by geography or type for the existing product line
Probable Consequences
- Increased sales volume

- Lowered unit costs if plant and distribution system are not already loaded

- Moderately increased profit margins

- Increased profit if new markets are growing more rapidly than existing markets

- Increased selling costs short-term

- Moderate improvement in cash flow

Requires:
- Modest capital investment (if new capacity needed)

- Increased working capital

Risk:
- High

E New Product/Same Market

To develop, broaden or replace products in the present product line selling them into the existing market served

Possible Consequences:
- Lowered unit costs if loaded into a plant with excess capacity

- Increased inventory

- Increased sales volume, profit and cash flow

- If a truly unique product, could provide new product margins which would tend to be considerably higher than from a mature product

Requires:
- Moderate new capital investment

- Increased development, design and manufacturing engineering

Risk:
- Moderate to high

F New Product/New Market

To invest in developing and marketing products related or unrelated to the present product line for new markets that are different in geography or by type from the present markets served by the business unit

Probable Consequences:
• Increased sales volume

• Increased costs initially

• Substantially increased profits if successful

• If products are unrelated to existing line, impact on performance will be like a new business

• If products are related to existing line, existing investment costs will be share, producing a higher initial profit

Requires:
• Increased working capital

• Possible increased capital investment

• Increased marketing and selling expenses

Risk:
• High (second only to initial market development)

G Backward Integration

To incorporate within the business organizational functions, operations or products that were previously external and that served to supply and support existing business operations

Probable Consequences:
• Reduced unit costs

• Secured supplies

• Somewhat increased margins

• Increased product line and sales volume if other than an entirely captive source

• May inhibit responsiveness to the marketplace because of a commitment to particular raw materials, components, or manufacturing process

Requires:
- Considerable capital investment

Risk:
- Moderate

H Forward Integration

To incorporate within the business organization functions between the current business and the ultimate consumer to that more effective distribution or increased control over the marketplace can be achieved

Probable Consequences:
- Increased sale from competitors' products already been handled by the distribution system

- Possibly reduced marketing cost

- Lower production costs because more stabilized production schedules are possible

- May increase total profits and return on investment

- Should produce higher returns than backward integration (unless tax and depreciation provisions greatly favor control over raw materials)

- Tendency to increase product line … to make full use of the distribution system

Requires:
- Increased capital (working and investment)

Risk:
- High (and considerably higher than backward integration sine both new products and new markets are involved

I Export / Same Product

To invest in marketing selected products of the domestic SBU to foreign markets …. these may or may not have the same competitors and market dynamics of the domestic market

Probably consequences:
- Increased sales volume

- Increased cash flow, long-term

- Increased profit margins in long-term

- Initially increased unit costs because of increased distribution and selling costs … possible decrease in unit costs because of increased volume (better utilization of facilities)

Requires:
- Increased marketing expense

- Increased working capital

Risk:
- Moderate to high

J Licensing Abroad
To exploit through licensing in foreign countries the use of domestic technology, patents, know-how, brand franchise, etc. belonging to the domestic business unit
Probable Consequences:
- Increased operating profit

- Increased cash flow

- Increased rate of return

Risk:
- Low to moderate because it is the lowest risk / lowest return of all of the overseas strategies

K Development of Overseas Production Facilities
To invest in offshore production plants for products to be sold in domestic markets by the domestic SBU
Probable Consequences:
- Considerably improved profit margins if located in a low cost country

- Substantially decreased operating costs in the long run

• Payouts as long-term with increased need for cash in the short-term

Requires:
• Increased capital expenditures

Risk:
• Low to moderate

L Development of Overseas Business
To establish overseas a separate SBU in the same industry as the domestic business unit, but in a market with different characteristics
Probable Consequences:
• Increased sales volume

• Lowered receivables and inventory in current business because of displacement

• Possible increased capacity

Requires:
• Capital investment

Risk:
• High, but moderated because of prior product and production experience

M Excess Capacity
To provide additional capacity for existing products beyond current needs … not incremental capacity … in order to meet anticipated future growth
Probable consequences:
• Improved capability to increase share of an increasing market

• Possible preclusion of competitors adding capacity

• Increased unit costs on the short term

• Negative impact on cash flow with no offsetting near-term benefits

Requires:
• Capital investment

Risk:
- Moderate to high since timing is critical

N Market Rationalization

To prune back the market served by the business unit to the most profitable segments and / or higher volume segments, or by particular type or geography, in order to concentrate marketing focus on the most profitable markets

Probable consequences:
- Initially reduced sales volume, but possible rebound with focused sales effort

- Increased profit margins

- Decreased working capital requirements because of decline in inventories

- Increased cash flow as a percent of sales

- Decline in receivables as a percent of sales

Requires:
- Courage

Risk:
- Moderate

O Distribution Rationalization

To prune back the distribution system to a more efficient network; this may include cutting back to the highest volume distributors or shaping by geography or type

Probable consequences:
- Increased profit margins following initial sales loss

- Lowered inventories

- Lowered distribution costs and investment

- Minor interruption in supply

Requires:
- Possible additional investment

Risk:
- Moderate since unit is giving up sales to a competitor

P Product Line Rationalization
To narrow the product line to the most profitable products
Probable consequences:
- Initial reduction in sales volume

- Improved working capital position

- Improved profitability

- Possible short-term under-utilization of assets

- Minor interruption in supply

Risk:
- Low to moderate

Q Production Rationalization
To increase standardization of designs, components, and manufacturing processes and / or concentrating facilities and / or subcontracting out elements of production
Probable Consequences:
- Lowered production costs

- Improved profit margin after initial displacement

- Improved working capital

- No impact on sales

- Minor interruption in supply

Requires:
- Some capital investment, increased manufacturing process engineering cost

Risk:
- Low to moderate

R Technological Efficiency

To improve operating efficiency through technological improvements in physical plant, systems and processes

Probable Consequences:

- Decreased variable costs and increased fixed costs resulting in an overall reduction

- Little effect on sales volume

Requires:
- Some capital investment

Risk:
- Low to moderate, depending on the extent to which the particular technology is proven

S Methods & Functions Efficiency

To invest in new ways of doing existing task by adding new "soft" technology, e.g., new patterns of work flow, computer-aided processing, so as to improve effectiveness and efficiency

Probable Consequences:
- Moderately improved operating performance

- Improve functional rather than product costs

Requires:
- Expense investment

Risk:
- Low to moderate

T Traditional Cost Cutting

To reduce costs uniformly through management edicts

Probable Consequences:
- Increased profit margins if the cost of administration and execution is reasonable

- Lowest possible return of all the various efficiency strategies

Requires:
- A responsive managerial system to implement management edicts with intelligence

Risk:
- Moderate since the arbitrary nature of the reductions may unforeseen results

U Hesitation

To slow down or establish a one-year moratorium on new capital investment and new expenses; it does not prohibit expense or capital investment for the normal maintenance of the business … e.g., because of capital limitations, dangers of overextending management or market uncertainties

Probable Consequences:
- No effect on short-term sales

- May disrupt multi-year facilities expansion program

- Competitive position may be weakened if program remains in place too long

- Decreased sales and earnings in long-term

Risk:
- Low, if relatively short-term

V Little Jewel

To strip down a business to the currently most profitable piece and reinvest the proceeds of the divestments in the successful operations retained

Probable Consequences:
- Decreased sales volume in the short run

- May produce underutilized capacity

- Increased RONA if assets are closed to being fully depreciated

- Decreased variable unit costs

Risk:
- Low

W Pure Survival

To maintain the existence of the business unit in periods of extremely adverse business conditions by eliminating functions products, or by under-financing any activity

Probable Consequences:

- Considerably decreased costs in the short run

- Markedly improved return on investment short-term

- Increased cash flow short-term

Risk:
- Moderate since risks long-term adverse effect on sales volume

X Unit Abandonment

To divest a business unit because of its inability to remain viable within the corporation or because the unit may be of greater value to someone else

Probable Consequences:

- Considerably decreased costs in the short run

- Markedly improved return on investment short-term

- Increased cash flow short-term

Risk:
- Moderate since company may have invested more in the assets that its market value

Note: Typically, this strategy applies most frequently to Embryonic (the good idea that wasn't) and Aging (market shrinking too fast)

Appendix 10

Getting Started List of Steps

1 Pick your leader and give that person the book so that they can prepare. They should be able to think on their feet, have some market experience, be respected by the other participants, and comfortable with approximations.

2 You and the leader pick the strategy development team. This should include everyone who will play a critical role in implementing the final strategy and a good balance of functional experience. Emphasize sales and marketing. Also include finance, HR, technology, production, R&D. When in doubt, be inclusive.

3 Poll team to find dates that work during the normal work week.

4 Set the date for the first working session (once you know the scope of the next steps, you can set the next date).

5 Make the onsite / offsite decision. If offsite, reserve the room, arrange for refreshments and food (getting out of the room for lunch is a fine idea), get comfortable chairs. Nothing turns off a group like folding metal chairs and a green baize covered table. Three days in a metal chair can dull the senses and paralyze the brain. In either case, arrange to have drafting tape, 2 large easel boards and magic markers in various colors available.

6 Issue the invitations and set up the ground rules. No ducking out other than for personal needs, no texting, leave the data books behind and do not bring these to the sessions, informal dress, etc.

7 Gather the materials for distribution at the appropriate time during the session. 1 copy for each participant and some spares of the forms from appendices 2, 3, 4, 5, 6, 7, 8, and 9.

8 Have someone check to make certain that the room is correctly set up about an hour before the session begins.

9 Make certain that the charts can be left up on the walls at the end of days 1 and 2. One time this wasn't done, and the hotel was used the room for another function. So all the charts were stripped off the walls and tossed. I spent the next early morning dumpster diving to get them back.

10 At the end of session gather all the materials, most particularly the charts and clean copies of any of the materials.

About the Author

Peter von Braun has spent most of his career developing and implementing strategic plans for a wide variety of situations. As a result, his system has been subjected to hundreds of real life tests. He has led strategy development teams in a wide variety of industries, as well as in many countries. These assignments included work in Argentina, Brazil, Canada, The Czech Republic, England, Egypt, France, Germany, Hong Kong, India, Italy, Japan, Mexico, Oman, Russia, Singapore, Spain, Switzerland, South Africa, the United States, Venezuela, and other countries.

He has carried out assignments for many types of companies ranging from those with sales of a few million to billions. These have included virtually everything from family owned companies to major public institutions. The industries cover the spectrum, with extensive experience in manufacturing, financial institutions, service industries, agriculture, health care and many others.

Following military service with both the U.S. Navy and Army, he graduated from Yale with High Honors in 3 years on the 250th anniversary of the first person in his family to graduate from Yale. He earned a Ph.D. summa cum laude from the University of Cologne in 2 years, where he was studying as a Fulbright Scholar. His thesis on strategy was chosen as one of the 6 books published annually by the German Government. Subsequently, he taught at Harvard Business School.

He became a partner at McKinsey & Co. in New York, where he stayed for 11 years, leaving as the result of a taxi accident, which kept him bed-ridden for the better part of a year.

In addition to creating his own strategy consulting practice, he was Chairman and CEO of several a private companies including the largest mineral micronutrient company in the U.S., an enhanced oil recovery company with operations in the USSR, India and other countries, and two biotechnology companies. The project in the USSR led to contacts at the highest level of government and provided a window on the breakup of the Soviet Union and the chaos that followed. He also created and was CEO of a company that successfully developed the noise abatement equipment allowing older 4-engine jet aircraft to meet strict Federal noise requirements.

He became deeply involved in economic development and public health campaigns. A major achievement stemmed from a project he created and led in the Sultanate of Oman where roughly 10% of the population was blind. The project focused on correction of remediable blindness as well as the research, curriculum, and system necessary conduct mass training in the prevention of blindness, for which he received a promotion in his order of knighthood from the Queen of England.

Another project on the coast of Labrador in Canada combined economic development and education. It involved rebuilding the coastal fishing industry in the area around Battle Harbour and creating a primary health care education system that transformed the ability of the people to provide critical services for themselves and their families in an area in which there were no medical professionals within hundreds of miles and one that often was weathered in for weeks at a time. This project spread to many other areas of northern Canada. During her visit to Canada, H.M. Queen Elizabeth II honored the project by a visit to its field headquarters, where Peter was presented to Her Majesty.

Just after the 1960s race riots in New York, Peter began working with the Congress of Racial Equality on a series of economic development projects. One of these focused on developing a system to accelerate reimbursement of Medicare and Medicaid receivables owed by New York City to Black-owned pharmacies in New York, which were being crippled by the inability of NYC to process reimbursements promptly and properly. A major loan-shark racket was victimizing these pharmacies, and led to the Empire State Pharmacy Association to begin organizing a boycott of both Medicare and Medicaid.

Peter organized and led the creation and implementation of a computer-based receivables processing system that received Federal and NY State sanction to operate. This system cut the reimbursement time from 9 – 15 months to two weeks and rejections from 40% to 50% to practically zero. The Bronx DA arrested several of the senior loan sharks and the city officials who cooperated with them, ending the organized crime exploitation of pharmacies.

He served for 7 years on the Vestry of Trinity Church, Wall Street, New York. He was on the Board of Directors of the Presiding Bishop's Fund for World Relief as well as serving as the Episcopal Church Representative to Church World Services. He was Chairman of the Battle Harbour Foundation.

This is Peter's 4th book. Previously, he published a the evolution of British Imperial defense strategy in India and Central Asia (Die Verteidigung Indiens), How to Save a Life, a book on primary health care, and How to Save an Eye, a book on preventive ophthalmology. These books appeared in English, German and Arabic. His articles have appeared in The Harvard Business Review, the Journal of Commerce, the New York Times, as well as other journals. He has testified twice before committees of the US Senate on national security issues and policy regarding the break-up of the Soviet Union.

Peter is married to Denene Jensen, and they have two children: Christina 20 and Alexander 19. The family commitment to winter sports comes from Denene, who was an instructor at Killington while in college and from Christina and Alexander, both of whom are committed snowboard competitors. Christina has ranked as high as #2 in the country in her age group and Alexander #1. Peter facilitates their interests in whatever way he can and tries to stay somewhat warm while doing it.

Peter can be reached at petervonbraun@verizon.net or by phone at 203 249 - 3782. His website (under construction) is www.plantowinbusinessstrategy.com